ITALY
BEFORE
ROME

The Making of the Past

ITALY
BEFORE
ROME

JOHN REICH

ELSEVIER ⊕ PHAIDON

For Barbara

Series Editor Graham Speake
Picture Editor Christine Forth
Design Gwyn Lewis
Production Ivor Parker
Index Scott Glover

Frontispiece: An Etruscan canopic urn from Chiusi. The stylized griffin
heads are borrowed from the Greek Orientalizing tradition and were
probably intended to be apotropaic (to avert evil). Museo Civico, Chiusi.

Elsevier-Phaidon, an imprint of Phaidon Press Ltd,
Littlegate House, St Ebbe's Street, Oxford

ISBN 0 7290 0075 3

Origination by E. Moffat & Company Ltd, High Wycombe, Bucks.
Filmset by Keyspools Ltd, Golborne, Lancs, England
Printed and bound by Brepols, Turnhout, Belgium

CONTENTS

PREFACE TO THE SERIES

This book is a volume in the Making of the Past, a series describing the early history of the world as revealed by archaeology and related disciplines. The series is written by experts under the guidance of a distinguished panel of advisers and is designed for the layman, for young people, the student, the armchair traveler and the tourist. Its subject is a new history – the making of a new past, uncovered and reconstructed in recent years by skilled specialists. Since many of the authors of these volumes are themselves practicing archaeologists, leaders in a rapidly changing field, the series is completely authoritative and up-to-date. Each volume covers a specific period and region of the world and combines a detailed survey of the modern archaeology and sites of the area with an account of the early explorers, travelers and archaeologists concerned with it. Later chapters of each book are devoted to a reconstruction in text and pictures of the newly revealed cultures and civilizations that make up the new history of the area.

Published titles

The Egyptian Kingdoms
The Aegean Civilizations
The Spread of Islam
The Emergence of Greece
The Rise of Civilization
The First Empires
Ancient Japan
Indian Asia
Ancient China

Biblical Lands
The New World
Man before History
The Greek World
Barbarian Europe
The Roman World
Rome and Byzantium
The Iranian Revival
Prehistoric Europe
The Kingdoms of Africa

INTRODUCTION

The achievements of Classical antiquity, Periclean Athens, for example, or the Rome of the Caesars, form the basis of the development of western civilization, and, since the Renaissance, scholars have studied their literary and material remains, helped in increasing measure by the development of the discipline of archaeology, in order to reach some understanding of their history and their culture. Many problems remain unsolved, and every year, as a result of new excavations or further research, old solutions are revised, but the general lines of the development of Classical Greece or Imperial Rome have by now been established. One of the reasons for the relative completeness of our picture of, say, Augustan Rome is of course the survival of a large body of literature, and the same applies to greater or lesser degree to almost all periods of Greek and Roman history from the time of Homer.

By the end of the 19th century a new interest had begun to develop about the world of the eastern Mediterranean before Homer, and the sensational finds at Mycenae and at Knossos formed the basis for our knowledge of Greece and the Aegean in the Bronze Age. In the past 60 years or so, discoveries in the field of Minoan and Mycenaean archaeology have produced a picture which, although far from complete, nevertheless provides a surprisingly detailed impression of life in the great Bronze Age centers of Crete and mainland Greece, in spite of the absence of contemporary historical accounts, and something at least – and often more than that – can be said about the history of the period.

To the west, however, things are very different. Not only is the prehistory of Italy still far from clearly understood, but our knowledge of even the later peoples of the Early Iron Age is extremely vague. The Etruscans themselves, the best-known of all non-Roman cultures in Italy, have become the archetypal "mysterious people," a reputation they still seem to retain in spite of the efforts of recent scholars to demythologize them; and other peoples, the Daunians, the Picenes and others, are barely known, still less understood. In many ways this is strange. The events in Italy with which this book deals took place within the lifetimes of most of the great historians of Classical times, from Herodotus to Polybius. The Etruscans were still around in the lifetime of Cicero or Livy, and Urganilla, the wife (for a time, at least) of the

Emperor Claudius, was herself an Etruscan who still spoke her own language – that language which remains among the most potent Etruscan "mysteries." How can it be that we know so much more about the Minoans of the early second millennium BC, who lived in an age from which no literature survives, than about a Villanovan or Messapian of 1,500 years later? One of the answers, of course, is that the Romanization of Italy obliterated much of the evidence for other cultures, and Roman writers continued the process of down-playing the achievements of their predecessors and contemporaries. This was partly for obvious political reasons, but partly also because, like their fellow Italians, the Romans fell under the spell of the Greeks and their art.

But thankfully the loss is not a permanent one, and the solution lies once again, as in the case of the Minoans, in the hands of the archaeologists. Recent excavations in Italy have shown how much evidence lies buried – literally – of the other cultures of Early Iron Age Italy. In the past 30 years there is perhaps no other aspects of Mediterranean archaeology in which so much new information has been acquired. The past ten years alone have seen important new evidence for the events surrounding the arrival of the Greeks in Campania in the 8th century, and for the history of Rome and the surrounding parts of Latium in the 7th century, and the discovery of a major Etruscan site of the 6th century at Murlo. We still cannot talk of being able to clarify our picture of the period, because there is still no general picture. The individual discoveries are of immense importance, but it will take time before they can be related to one another and before a coherent account emerges of life in Italy before the period of Roman domination. Nonetheless, the prospects are extremely hopeful.

This book attempts to summarize some of the more recent finds and developments and to provide a connected account of them. As such, it is of course very much an interim report, inevitably outdated by the excavations of this year or next, and equally inevitably, it sidesteps many of the detailed problems which at present concern professionals in the field – the early history of Rome, the problems of Villanovan chronology, and others. If nothing else, however, it may serve to introduce the reader to a number of peoples and cultures that were responsible for producing some of the most striking ancient works of art.

CHRONOLOGICAL TABLE

BC	NORTHERN ITALY	CENTRAL ITALY AND SARDINIA	SOUTHERN ITALY AND SICILY	ELSEWHERE IN THE MEDITERRANEAN
900	Villanovan I at Bologna Este I in the Veneto	Villanovan I at Tarquinia Full Nuraghic culture in Sardinia		Geometric period in Greek art **814** Foundation of Carthage
800	Villanovan I at Bologna	**753** Foundation of Rome	Villanovan tombs at Pontecagnano Beginnings of Picene and Apulian cultures	
750	Este II Ligurian cemetery at Chiavari	Villanovan II at Tarquinia Earliest appearance of Etruscan culture	The Greeks arrive in Ischia **706** Foundation of Taranto	Homer (?) Orientalizing period in Greek art
700	Villanovan III at Bologna	Growth of Tarquinia and Cerveteri	Oscan foundation of Pompeii	
650		**616** Etruscan kings at Rome Portonaccio temple constructed at Veii		**612** Fall of Nineveh
600	Este III	Greek colony founded near Tarquinia at Gravisca	Foundation of Capua (?)	Archaic period in Greek art **574** Defeat of Phoenician Empire by Assyrians
550	Growth of Spina	Earliest surviving painted tomb at Tarquinia **540** Etruscans and Carthaginians defeat Greeks at Alalia **525** Destruction of Murlo **510** Etruscans expelled from Rome Carthaginians arrive in Sardinia	**524** Failure of Etruscan attack on Greece **511** Sybaris destroyed by Croton	**525–404** Persians ruling in Egypt
500	Etruscans arrive in Bologna Foundation of Marzabotto	**499** Battle of Lake Regillus **493** Treaty between Rome and Latins	**480** Carthaginians defeated at Himera **478** Hieron becomes king at Syracuse **474** Etruscans defeated at Carine	**496** Ionian revolt **490** Battle of Marathon **480–479** First defeat of Xerxes by Greeks at battles of Salamis and Plataea Classical period in Greek art
450	Arrival of Celts (?)		**438** Samnite conquest of Capua (?) **421** Samnite conquest of Cumna **415–413** Athenian expedition to Syracuse **405** Dionysius I becomes king of Syracuse Samnite conquest of Poseidonia	**431–404** Peloponnesian war
400	**396** Sack of Melpum	**396** Fall of Veii **390** Gallic sack of Rome **353** Peace between Rome and Cerveteri **351** Peace between Rome and Tarquinia		
350	Gallic occupation of Bologna	**325–290** Samnite wars **321** Samnite defeat of Romans at Caudine Forks		**336** Death of Philip of Macedon Succeeded by Alexander **323** Death of Alexander Hellenistic period in Greek art
300		**280** Vulci conquered by Rome	**273** Poseidonia becomes a Roman colony, renamed Paestum	

Opposite: Painted terracotta ash urn from Chiusi. The subject of the relief is the fight between Eteocles and Polyneices. Note the libation cup, or patera, in the right hand of the figure on the top and the well-preserved paint. British Museum, London.

1 ITALY BEFORE THE IRON AGE

Most of this book will be concerned with the peoples and cultures of Italy in the Early Iron Age. Some of them developed on Italian soil, like the Etruscans or the Samnites, while others, like the Greeks and the Carthaginians, by establishing colonies in Italy, brought new ideas from abroad. These immensely varied cultures, existing side by side throughout Italy, from the Alps to Sicily, are fascinating in themselves as well as important for the way in which they help in the understanding of by far the best-known people of ancient Italy, the Romans. Roman pride in their own achievements led the Romans to minimize their dependence on those Italic peoples whom they themselves had conquered, and emphasize their own uniqueness, but the Eternal City itself began its history as just another Latin village in a country culturally dominated by Italic tribes like the Picenes, the Umbrians and others, and by the Etruscans; a country into which the Greeks were introducing new ideas from the east. After looking at the range of these cultures of Iron Age Italy, therefore, we shall see, in a final chapter, something of their effect on Rome.

But the history of early Italy begins long before the Iron Age, and this first chapter is concerned with the earliest life there. Italy's position in the center of the Mediterranean basin has always attracted settlers, and already by 200,000 BC early man had arrived in many parts of the peninsula. The position and geography of Italy were always to play a large part in its history. To the north the Alps divide it from the rest of Europe, but they can be crossed by a number of good passes, some of which were in use from the Neolithic period, while even earlier some of the first settlers had discovered that the value of the Alpine mineral resources compensated for their inaccessibility. South of the Alps extends the vast plain of the Po valley, broad and almost entirely flat, and made fertile by the rivers which descend southward from the mountains to the north, and in many cases flow directly into the river Po itself. But the richness of the earth in this great valley, which has attracted settlers of all periods, and is now one of Italy's chief farming areas, is counterbalanced by the danger of flooding and by the large tracts of marshland on the east coast around the Po delta: when the Etruscans began to expand northward in the 6th century BC they probably began to drain them, but much of the Po delta has only been habitable since the last century. The continual flooding which must have made life so uncertain for the early farmers of the Po valley has not helped archaeologists either: one of its results is that the silt, which overflowed on to the land along with the water, has covered many of the earliest sites throughout the plain to such a depth that, even if they are ever actually found, they have become almost impossible to excavate, and even Roman remains are in places buried more than 30 feet deep.

To the south, the rest of continental Italy is distinguished and unified by

The Mediterrranean world.

the presence throughout of two elements: mountains and sea. It is surrounded on three sides by the Mediterranean, and the Apennine mountains, which cut it off from northern Italy to the south of the Po valley, run meanderingly all the way to the southern tip, across from the straits of Messina and the northwest corner of Sicily. But although there is nowhere else on the peninsula a fertile plain comparable in size to that of the valley of the Po, the Apennines are rarely sufficiently high or impassable to prevent communication, and much of the land, although hilly, can easily be cultivated. The rolling landscape of Tuscany has always attracted settlers, from Neolithic man to Elizabeth Barrett Browning, and its striking natural beauty is supplemented by the extremely rich mineral deposits of southern Tuscany and Elba. Further south, both Latium and Campania have coastal plains which, once drained, were cultivated, and inland valleys whose soil is enriched by the minerals from extinct volcanoes along the west coast: a string of these once existed, although now only Vesuvius is still active. On the Adriatic coast a narrow open strip runs continuously down past the spur of Italy's boot to the heel, a relatively flat area with cultivable land, while inside the heel is the fine natural harbor where the city of Taranto was to develop and play an important part in connecting Italy with foreign influences. Only the tip of the peninsula,

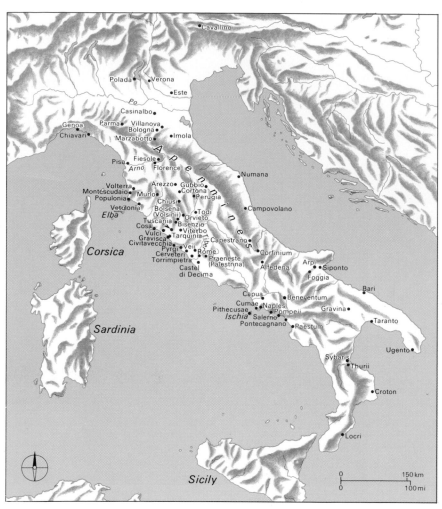

Above: Footprint of one of the first Italians. It was made by a specimen of Neanderthal man in the wet clay floor of the Grotta della Basura in Liguria. Length c. 21 cm.

Above right: The principal sites of ancient Italy.

modern Basilicata and Calabria, does not share in these abundances: the soil is poor, inland communications are difficult, and there are few mineral resources to compensate. But across the straits of Messina, easily visible on a clear day, there lies Sicily, whose rich land has been coveted and won by an almost unending procession of foreign invaders over the past 4,000 years, and whose position has always made it a natural point of communication both between the eastern and western Mediterranean and between Europe and Africa. Italy's other large island, Sardinia, is more mountainous and less accessible as it lies off the main sailing routes, both ancient and modern. We shall see something of its culture in the Bronze Age and Early Iron Age, the only period during which it produced an independent culture. Sardinia's main importance lay in its silver and iron mines which were to become in the 7th and 6th centuries BC a point of contention between Etruscans, Carthaginians and Greeks.

Italy in the Stone Age. By the Lower Paleolithic Age, man had arrived in Italy, probably during one of the warm periods in this age of glaciations. Nothing has been found of human remains from this remote period (about 200,000 BC), but some of the tools used by these first Italians, who probably belonged to the *Homo erectus* type, have survived, including hand axes which have been found near Verona and to the south of the Po valley, near Imola. Near Rome itself, at Torrimpietra, a Lower Paleolithic settlement has been excavated, with traces of hearths and huts, and animal bones left over from meals, together with the hand axes probably used to carve up the

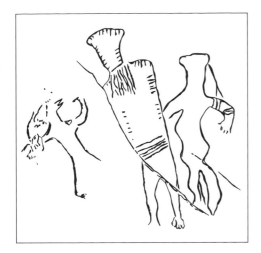

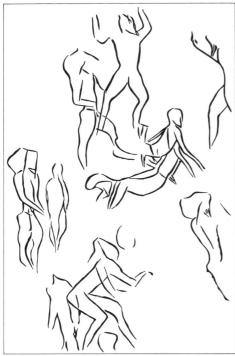

Top: These incised figures were discovered in 1950 on the wall of a cave at Cala dei Genovesi, on the island of Levanzo. The middle one, which seems to be bearded, is about 30 cm high. After Brea.

Above: Paleolithic cave drawing from Addaura, just outside Palermo. The figures are deeply incised and average 25 cm in height; they seem to be taking part in a ritual dance around two prisoners or sacrificial victims. The vitality of several of the dancers gives them a Matisse-like quality.

carcasses of the animals which had provided the food.

By 60,000 BC, the approximate beginning of the Middle Paleolithic period, man had developed into a new type, *Homo neanderthalis*, chiefly represented in Italy by flint scrapers and points, although two of them have left us their footprints, preserved in the clay floor of a cave in Liguria. For millennia life must have been almost entirely occupied with the struggle for survival and the search for food, and Neanderthal man probably existed on a diet of birds and fish, the few larger mammals he could find and trap including goats, deer and even bear, and roots and berries. But in the midst of this precarious existence there occurred a major development in the pattern of human behavior, for Neanderthal man was the first human to bury his dead in graves and cemeteries; and traces of Middle Paleolithic cemeteries have been found in caves to the south of Rome. It is difficult for us to imagine what processes of thought or belief led to this break with the past, but it suggests a new concern with values other than mere survival.

It was only at the beginning of the Upper Paleolithic period, around 30,000 BC, that man first crossed the straits of Messina and arrived in Sicily. Thereafter, throughout the end of the Paleolithic Age and the succeeding Mesolithic period, Sicily attracted increasing numbers of settlers, particularly in the beautiful coastal area around the modern city of Palermo, known as the Conca d'Oro (the Golden Horn), and from there came the first notable works of art to be produced on Italian soil. In general, Paleolithic art is much better represented elsewhere in Europe, notably in the great caves of Lascaux in France and Altamira in Spain, but in 1950 both painted and incised animals and human figures were found in a cave on the island of Levanzo, just off the west coast of Sicily, followed three years later by the discovery of the Paleolithic cave drawings at Addaura. In one of these caves, which lie on the northern slopes of Monte Pellegrino just outside Palermo itself, some bombs had been stored during World War II and forgotten, and their sudden accidental explosion stripped off parts of the thick layer of incrustation which had formed over the wall: underneath lay some of the most vivid and lively of all Paleolithic art. The drawings, which include humans and animals, fall into three groups, of which one is especially detailed and impressive, showing what seems to be a ritual dance or ceremony. In the center of a circle of dancing men are two male figures lying on the ground, apparently tied up: one of them seems to have his feet tied to his neck, with his legs bent back, and the other, although less carefully drawn, seems to show a similar contortion. Both men are ithyphallic, and some scholars have interpreted the scene as one of sacrifice or torture, the men's condition being produced by strangulation; others have suggested that it may represent a ceremony of sexual initiation. The figures who form the circle around are all naked; their dance is characterized by lively, even violent, hand and body movements, although the hands themselves, like the feet, are not drawn in. But while the bodies are treated naturalistically, the faces have no features indicated, and in some cases seem to be covered with a bird-head mask. Elsewhere in the same scene a single hunter is shown in pursuit of a deer which seems to be galloping up a slope.

Much about these drawings remains mysterious, including their date, but even if we shall probably never come closer to understanding precisely what the scene represents, it provides a rare and precious insight into the world of Paleolithic man. Elsewhere in Italy it is not until 5000 BC and the beginning of the Neolithic period that life seems to have moved beyond the

Most of the painted figures in the Genovesi cave are represented schematically, but this little seated figure (its height is about 30 cm) is surprisingly naturalistic. It is painted in red, unlike the others which are black.

level of previous millennia. Around 7000 BC new skills in agriculture and the domestication of animals and the new craft of pottery manufacture had begun to develop further east in Greece and Asia Minor; and around 5000 BC the first of the many waves of immigrants who were, over the centuries, to change Italian life, sailed west to the east coast of Italy, bringing their newly developed techniques with them. Their arrival, coupled with the effects of increasing trade contacts and the new agricultural techniques, made it possible for Neolithic man, instead of ceaselessly wandering in search of food, to stay in one place, cultivate crops and breed domestic animals, and establish some sort of permanent community. And while the men in the settlements turned from hunting to farming, the women could devote themselves to the making of pottery, developing attractive styles of decoration which could be appreciated at leisure in the new domestic tranquillity. The effects of these changes can be seen throughout Italy during the Neolithic period. In the plain of the Tavoliere in Apulia almost 300 villages were established, some of them of considerable size, surrounded by defensive ditches whose presence suggests that life was not altogether idyllic in Neolithic Italy: although weapons are rarely found in sites of the period, these ditches and the stone walls which often accompany them seem to show a wish, if not a need, for defense against outsiders, whether from nearby villages or from abroad. Further north, in Emilia and in Liguria, Neolithic houses and pottery have been found, and at Molino Casarotto in the Veneto a joint excavation of the universities of Ferrara and Birmingham has uncovered one of the settlements of a culture whose chief characteristic is their manufacture of square-mouthed pottery; a number of houses were found collected together in groups, perhaps for security, with wooden floors and stone hearths.

The Copper Age. Although already by the late Neolithic period metal objects were being imported from abroad, it was only at the end of the third millennium BC that the use of metal became widespread in Italy, and this major cultural break was once again caused by the arrival of fresh waves of immigrants, this time predominantly from north of the Alps. The newcomers, who settled throughout north and central Italy, brought with them not only new technical skills, but a far less peaceful way of life, and many of the copper objects found in their settlements were weapons – daggers, halberds and battle-axes. In the tombs of the period, in which a number of members of the same family were buried together, copper weapons are frequently found left alongside the bodies of the dead whose property they presumably were. Apart from these cemeteries, little evidence has survived of the way of life of these people, but it is clear that the mineral resources of southern Tuscany, which were to play an important part in the later Villanovan and Etruscan periods, were discovered at a relatively early date, leading to the setting up of local forges and workshops.

Meanwhile to the south, where no tombs have yet been found, and the only evidence comes from habitation sites, the picture is typical of Italy throughout the subsequent Bronze and Iron Ages: each region seems to have developed along its own lines, reacting to foreign influences in its own way and using them to meet its own needs. This probably suggests that the times were too disturbed to allow a single culture to grow and spread in peace, but cultural diversity, as we shall find again and again, is an Italian characteristic. By the beginning of the Bronze Age this fragmentation had

Above: View of Lake Garda. The mild climate around the lake and the availability of food within it served to attract settlers from the early Neolithic period. A number of square-mouthed-pottery settlements have been excavated around the southern tip, not far from the later lake village of Polada, which dates to the Early Bronze Age.

Left: Square-mouthed pottery beakers: the one on the left from Molino Casarotto, near Vicenza, height 11 cm; on the right from San Germano, near Vicenza, height 18 cm. This style of pottery is typical of a culture which began to develop in northern Italy shortly after 4000 BC and lasted most of the next 1,000 years in a variety of forms. Examples are also found in Liguria, but those from the Veneto are generally better made and often decorated.

intensified throughout Italy and sophisticated northern lake villages like Polada on Lake Garda have little in common with settlements in the south, where life reverted to the level of Neolithic days.

The lake villages are among the best-known and most interesting sites from this period anywhere in Europe, mainly because the water on the edge of which they were built has preserved types of material that elsewhere have vanished, so that we can form a surprisingly complete picture of life in them. The villages were built on wooden platforms, and their inhabitants pursued a wide range of occupations. Fishing was popular, as can be seen from the dug-out canoes found at many of the sites, together with wooden floats from fishing nets. Farmers had a wide range of tools available, including the plow and sickle, and the average diet must have been varied in comparison with earlier periods. Indeed in the long and rich history of Italian cooking, the Polada culture deserves at least an honorable mention. As well as fish and freshwater turtles, the meat available included beef, pork and lamb, and whisks, sieves and the recent discovery of what

Above: So-called Baton of Command. One of four similar objects made from antlers, which were found in the grave of a young man buried in the cave of Arene Candide in Liguria, dating to the Upper Paleolithic period. Their name derives from the fact that they were originally thought to be symbols of authority, although this is far from certain. Museo Archeologico di Pegli, Genoa.

Above right: View of the site of the Early Bronze Age village at Molina on the small lake of Ledro, at the northwestern end of Lake Garda. Large numbers of wooden piles were discovered on the shoreline, either to support a platform on which the village was built, or to strengthen the bank of the lake.

Right: Dugout canoe carved from an oak trunk, found at the Early Bronze Age lake village of Lucone on the western shore of Lake Garda. The hole in the carved prow probably served to hold a mooring rope.

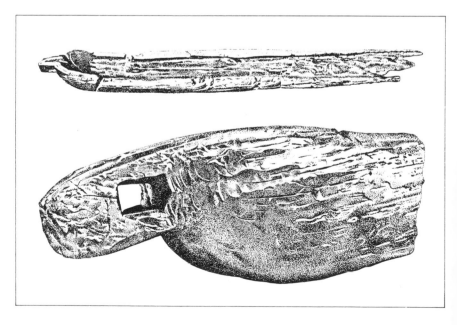

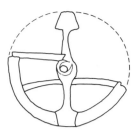

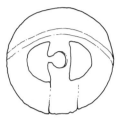

may be a churn at one of the villages suggest that butter and cheese were probably made. These were supplemented by wheat and barley, and by wild fruits like apples, strawberries, raspberries and plums. Even more intriguingly, at the village of Ledro were found the carbonized remains of what was probably a loaf of bread, and small balls of dough bearing a strong resemblance to the *gnocchi* or dumplings eaten today in Italy. And, as if this were not varied enough, wild game was also hunted, and the Early Bronze Age housewife could include in her menus venison, wild boar and game birds. Life was not restricted to agriculture or hunting either. Finds of molds, crucibles and bellows nozzles show that the craft of metalworking was well developed, and in almost every village there is evidence of spinning and weaving. Loom weights and spindle whorls are commonly found, and even some fragments of embroidered cloth have survived. Many of these technological innovations came from north of the Alps, and never made their way south of the Po, so that the sophistication of the Polada culture was limited to a small area; further south, life was still both more primitive and more disturbed.

The Middle Bronze Age which followed, as we shall see in a subsequent chapter, was to bring to southern Italy a new cultural unity in the period dominated by the Apennine culture, and developments from this led in turn to the Iron Age. But before plunging into the complex history of continental Italy in the last stages of the Bronze Age, this is the time to see something of Bronze Age life in Sicily and Sardinia, which in both islands reached a high cultural level in this period, in the case of Sardinia for the only time in its history.

Bronze Age Sicily. The people who brought metal to Sicily sometime after 3000 BC came not from mainland Italy but probably from Anatolia and the islands of the eastern Mediterranean, and carried with them a culture far more sophisticated than anything previously known so far in the west. Not only did they know how to work in bronze, but also in gold, silver and lead; they came not from simple villages, but from towns with public buildings for storing grain, wells, and paved squares and streets. Most important of all, in terms of their effect upon the west, they knew how to construct boats capable of long voyages by open sea, by which they could not only reach all parts of Sicily and the small islands around it, but could sail as far as southern France and even Spain, and there is evidence of trade both to and from the newly developing western regions. As in mainland Italy, Sicily shows wide local variations of culture, but everywhere the new ideas produced a high level of creativity. South and southeast Sicily were dominated in the Early Bronze Age by a culture named for the village of Castelluccio, where at the end of the 19th century a settlement of the period was excavated, and here, as later in the Bronze Age, we can see the Sicilian preoccupation with death and burial. In a valley near where the village stood, hundreds of tombs were cut in the rock, each one consisting of a separate chamber in some cases preceded by a small anteroom, closed either by a wall or by a carved stone slab decorated with spiral designs. The designs are reminiscent of similar ones in the Minoan art of Crete, and show how much Sicily owed to the eastern Mediterranean in the Early Bronze Age. They also have a parallel in the carvings of the temple of Tarxien on Malta, of a few centuries earlier, suggesting to archaeologists a possible connection between the Castelluccio culture and Malta. These theories were confirmed in 1964, when a Maltese

Wooden wheels from Mercurago, to the southwest of Lake Maggiore: they date either to the Early or Middle Bronze Age phase of the village there. One of them is solid, made of three planks, and the other is spoked: if it belongs to the Early Bronze Age, it is one of the earliest examples of a spoked wheel in Europe. After Barfield.

Two-handled pot from Molina di Ledro. The elbow-shaped handles and the simple relief decoration are characteristic of pottery from Early Bronze Age lake villages. Museo Nazionale, Trentino.

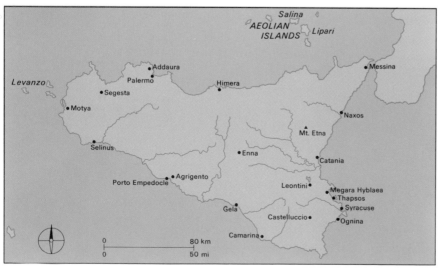

Above: A view of Mount Etna which shows the rich agricultural land surrounding the base of the volcano. A number of Neolithic villages (of a cultural type known as Stentinello) have been excavated on the southern slopes of Etna.

Left: Sicily.

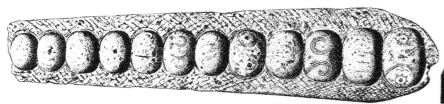

trading post was found at Ognina on the coast to the south of Syracuse, with large quantities of Maltese pottery.

Each of the burial chambers of the Castelluccio cemetery was used to hold several bodies, often accompanied by grave goods, and these include objects which demonstrate the spread of Sicily's growing contacts with the outside world. A number of the tombs contained long plaques of bone decorated with bosses and elaborate designs, finely shaped and carved, which may have had a religious significance, although their exact purpose is unknown. Almost identical plaques have also been found on Malta, in mainland Italy, in the Peloponnese at Lerna, and even at Troy; so that by the Early Bronze Age Sicily was already in contact with a far wider range of cultural influences than mainland Italy, and these were to increase.

Throughout the Middle Bronze Age (about 1400–1200 BC) the entire Mediterranean was dominated by the Mycenaeans, a people "rich in gold," as Homer called them, with their great fortress citadels in the Peloponnese. Mycenaean wealth and influence were derived to a great extent from trade, and their routes extended as far west as Spain and as far north as England, where a gold cup and a sword of Mycenaean type were found in the grave of a Wessex chieftain. It was natural that in their journeys west the Mycenaeans would establish contacts with Italy, and, as we shall see in a later chapter, the chief base for their trade there was Taranto, but it is in Sicily that their influence was the strongest. According to the traditional legends Sicily is even linked to the Mycenaeans' predecessors, the Minoans of Crete, since none other than King Minos himself died there. The story goes that Daedalus, the Athenian craftsman in King Minos' service, left Crete against his master's wishes and fled to Sicily. Minos pursued him there, and discovered him at Inkyon, where he had constructed the fortress of Kamikos for the local king, Kokalos. When Minos demanded that Daedalus be handed over to him, Kokalos, not wishing to betray his guest,

Above: One of the decorated door slabs from the necropolis at Castelluccio, now in the Syracuse Museum. These carved slabs are the only examples of stone-carving so far discovered in prehistoric Sicily. A number of them are decorated with versions of the spiral motif, in a style reminiscent of earlier carvings found on Malta.

Top left: Near the village of Castelluccio, hundreds of rock tombs were carved into the limestone cliffs. They date to 1800–1400 BC, and consist of small oval chambers, the entrances to which are often closed by door slabs. The height of the doorways is generally about 1 m. Within each tomb several bodies had been buried, and in some cases the burials were sufficiently undisturbed for the excavators to be able to recover the grave goods. After Noto.

Below left: This bone plaque, decorated with bosses, comes from the necropolis at Castelluccio, and measures c. 16 cm in length. Other very similar objects have been found outside Sicily, including examples from Lerna in the Peloponnese and Troy, providing an important link between Sicily and the Aegean.

Above: Two gold finger rings from Pantalica, the larger of which is c.2 cm in diameter. They were found in the Late Bronze Age cemetery there (c.1250–1000 BC) and seem to show evidence of Mycenaean influence.

Opposite: Pottery forms from Bronze Age Sicily. The small goblet is Mycenaean, and shows a typical elegance of shape and decoration. The larger piece is about 32 cm high and comes from Thapsos. It consists of a small bowl on a high stand, inside which is a smaller bowl, and may possibly have been used as a lamp, perhaps in imitation of the stone lamps used in the Minoan palaces. Museo Archeologico, Agrigento.

especially having just benefited from his expert skill, delayed Minos long enough to persuade him to take a bath, in which Kokalos' daughters promptly drowned him in boiling water. Kokalos handed over Minos' body to the Cretans saying that their king had died accidentally, and they buried him near Agrigento, where his grave was still shown to travelers in Classical times, and constructed a temple to Aphrodite as a memorial. (Kokalos' memorial, incidentally, is an important journal of Sicilian archaeology which has been named for him.)

The legend is a strange one. Whereas on the one hand there is little or no archaeological evidence to show that the Minoans were ever in Sicily, the description of Minos' tomb given by the Greek historian Diodorus Siculus corresponds to an astonishing degree with the plan of the so-called Temple Tomb excavated earlier this century at Knossos. If there really was a shrine of the sort to be seen in Sicily – and all traces of it have now disappeared – some contact with Minoan Crete must have existed. About Mycenaean influences, at any rate, there can be no doubt: Mycenaean pottery, jewelry and weapons have all been found there, for the most part in the southeast corner of Sicily itself and on the little cluster of islands known as the Aeolian islands off its north coast. The best-preserved site of the period is at Thapsos, on the coast near modern Syracuse, where the shore and the cliffs along it are lined with hundreds of tombs cut into the rock, some on the upper level with steps leading vertically down into the cliff itself and others hollowed out of the side of the rock. In the tombs had been buried, along with the dead, pottery of Mycenaean manufacture or style.

Finds like this pottery, or the Egyptian-type faience beads found on Salina, one of the Aeolian islands, show that, unlike the rest of Italy, Sicily continued to develop trade contacts with the world of the eastern Mediterranean throughout the Middle Bronze Age. Further discoveries at Thapsos in recent years have shown that the contacts were not merely superficial, and that Mycenaean ideas had made a strong impact on the Sicilian way of life. From an archaeological point of view, it must be remembered, objects can be bought and sold and styles initiated without necessarily implying a fundamental cultural relationship: the Oriental rugs in many modern European and American homes do not mean that their owners have adopted a Turkish or Persian life-style. But when the plan and buildings of an entire town are affected, clearly the cultural influences are much stronger; and recent excavations have shown that Thapsos, while never a Mycenaean colony, was converted under Mycenaean influence from a settlement of round huts to a well-laid-out town, with rectilinear streets, containing large building complexes, where rooms were placed around a central paved courtyard in a way reminiscent of the Mycenaean palaces of Pylos, Tiryns and Mycenae itself. There is nothing on the mainland of Italy that equals this level of sophistication.

But by the Late Bronze Age, around 1200 BC, the disturbances in the eastern Mediterranean, which are reflected in the sack of Troy and the subsequent fall of the Mycenaeans, had begun to affect Sicily powerfully enough to break up the prosperous communities which had been established, and drive their inhabitants from the coast to the rugged interior of the island. The peace of earlier days was gone, and the subsequent disturbances and confusion lasted for almost 500 years, a true Sicilian dark age. The cultural developments and movements during this period are immensely complex and often difficult to follow on the basis of the evidence we have: the major difficulties lie in reconciling the archaeologi-

cal picture with the accounts provided by Greek historians, who claim that when the first Greeks arrived in Sicily towards the end of the 8th century BC, they found two races, the Sikels and Sikanians. The Sikanians, the original inhabitants of Sicily, had been attacked around the 11th century BC by the Sikels, who came from mainland Italy, and driven into the south and west of the island. If this account were true, the culture of the period immediately before the arrival of the Greeks should have something in common with those of the mainland, the late Apennine and proto-Villanovan cultures, which will be discussed in a later chapter. In fact, apart from the Aeolian islands and the coast opposite, nowhere in Sicily is there any evidence for mainland influence: Sicilian culture seems to have retained its links with the eastern Mediterranean. It is probably true to say, therefore, that when the first Greek colonizers arrived in Sicily any Italian invaders had long since been absorbed into the native peoples, and the Greeks found a culture that had far more in common with their own than with the mainland.

The history of Sicily shows, of course, many periods of brilliant cultural achievement alternating with times of poverty and oppression, and the events of the Bronze Age seem to foreshadow later cultures which developed there under the inspiration of foreign ideas, only to be submerged by a fresh wave of invaders, who later absorbed what they came to destroy. Phoenicians, Greeks, Romans, Goths, Arabs, Normans, Spaniards, all have been attracted by the climate and position of an island whose beauties and advantages have all too often, alas, brought it suffering. If its first great period of prosperity has left little permanent impression, in comparison with later periods, at least it was not entirely forgotten. Professor Bernabò Brea, one of the most distinguished figures in the history of Sicilian archaeology, has pointed out the way in which memories of Mycenaean voyages to Sicily are preserved in the legends which form part of the *Odyssey*. For the Mycenaeans, Sicily was a rich and mysterious country, guarded to the north by the two monsters Scylla and Charybdis. Around it floated the island of Aeolia, surrounded by a bronze wall, ruled over by Aeolus, the king of the winds, and on its east coast Odysseus and his men finally landed to their great relief, after passing through the straits of Messina. "When we had escaped from the rocks and terrible Charybdis and Scylla, we landed on the sun god's honored island, where his fine broad-browed cattle and fat sheep wander."

Sardinia and Nuraghic culture. The strange and impressive Nuraghic culture of Sardinia, so-called for its most visible monuments, the huge stone-built forts and towers known as *nuraghi*, began to develop during the last part of the Bronze Age, and continued down to the arrival of the Romans in the 3rd century BC. For much of its history, therefore, we shall be moving ahead into a period later than the events described so far in this chapter, into the Iron Age; but Nuraghic culture has a unity of its own, and in any case well into the Iron Age the Nuraghic people were still using bronze as their principal metal. This cultural isolation is typical: throughout its early history Sardinia had little contact with Italy or anywhere else. Unlike Sicily, it does not lie on the main shipping routes to the west, so that eastern merchants were not likely to call there, and even from Italy it lies many hours' sail distant, across open water. The nearest point of land is the island of Corsica, itself almost as isolated, and to the west are the Balearic islands and Spain. It is not surprising, therefore, that the

earliest cultures to develop in Sardinia had links with the Iberian peninsula as well as with Italy and the eastern Mediterranean, and even these first signs of life appeared at a comparatively late date. There is no evidence that man arrived there much before 2000 BC, and the first villages and cemeteries show a combination of western-type pottery and eastern-style burial customs: the pots in use included beakers and other vessels of a kind characteristic of the Pyrenees and southwest France, while the rock-cut tombs were similar to those we have seen in Sicily, and almost certainly imitated from eastern Mediterranean examples, perhaps by way of Sicily itself. In terms of eastern influence, even more striking is the similarity between the fertility idols of the Cycladic islands in the Aegean and early statuettes found in Sardinia, which probably represent a female divinity: the Sardinian examples are of local stone, and so not imported, and suggest not only artistic but also religious connections with the Minoan world, perhaps involving the cult and worship of a mother goddess. We shall find later evidence that tends to support this.

Three fertility idols. The crudest, the so-called Venus of Savignano (*far left*), is of a type familiar in the eastern Mediterranean from the Neolithic period, represented in Sardinia by the Venus from Macomer. Contacts between Sardinia and the Aegean are further illustrated by the other two: the idol from Senorbi (*above left*) is clearly related to the familiar Cycladic type (*above*), although it is more stylized. Analysis of the marble has proved, however, that the stone is local. Museo Pigorini, Rome, and British Museum, London.

The first Sardinian culture died out around 1500 BC, and shortly after, the earliest Nuraghic buildings began to be constructed. The word *nuraghe* is of uncertain origin. The Greeks, who loved to derive words from proper names, believed that the buildings were named for their legendary constructor, Norax, founder of the city of Nora, but the word probably derives from a local term meaning oddly enough either "pile" or "hollow." The *nuraghi* were constructed of huge blocks of irregular stones fitted closely together without mortar, and the earliest examples had a single round central chamber roofed over by a corbeled vault. Around the inside, niches were cut at ground level for beds, and in some cases terraces and upper stories were added. The large number of these *nuraghi* still standing in Sardinia – well over 6,000 have been found and many more have probably been destroyed or have collapsed – means that their use was not confined to the ruling class, although some of the larger complexes which developed at a later date were probably intended as fortresses for warrior chieftains. The simpler ones must have served as farmhouses for individual families and in some regions groups of several *nuraghi* were built close together, to form a trading settlement, although even in these cases defense played an important part in their design and construction. The upper stories were approached by stairways which were left dark and often did not lead directly up, so that any stranger would find access to the upper regions difficult. Life in Sardinia in the Late Bronze Age must have been extremely unsettled, with the continuous threat of war, to have required buildings like these, and we shall find that Nuraghic art confirms their rather grim quality.

By 1000 BC Sardinia was becoming more drawn into contact with other Mediterranean civilizations, and in the following centuries the Phoenicians, attracted by the island's mineral resources, established a series of peaceful trading settlements in coastal regions. At the same time the designs of the *nuraghi* became far more elaborate as the native population became richer and more sophisticated. Additional rooms and towers were added to already existing buildings and some complexes were surrounded by an outside wall. The Nuraghe Sant'Antine is a good example of this rebuilding: a tower three stories high was built over an earlier structure in the 9th century BC, and a century later three other towers were added, linked by a wall which encloses an inner courtyard. In the case of the elaborate *nuraghe* at Barumini the construction was even more intricate and the finished building was protected by a series of massive walls, which in places enclose some of the huts of the surrounding village.

It is clear that by the 6th century BC these great complexes were primarily intended for defense against invaders from the Phoenician colony of Carthage, whose interest in the Sardinian mines was no doubt augmented by their knowledge that it was shared by the Greeks. The message was not lost on the Sardinians: precautions were taken against siege, the entrances of the *nuraghi* were made as inaccessible as possible, and in the larger ones wells were dug within the walls to provide a water supply for the beleaguered inhabitants. It says much for the Carthaginian forces that by the end of the 6th century BC they had been able to sack and destroy many of the *nuraghi* and take over much of the island, driving the native Nuraghic people underground. From then on Sardinia became dominated by foreign cultures, Carthaginian, Greek and Etruscan, and by the end of the 3rd century BC had passed into Roman hands following the First Punic War.

If our picture of the people who built the *nuraghi* had to be derived only from the buildings themselves, it would be difficult to form much of an impression of them. Fortunately they have left us a large number of bronze figurines, mostly dating to the 8th to 6th centuries BC, which bring their culture startlingly to life, with their combination of gauntness and expressivity. Many of them confirm our impression that the Nuraghic culture centered around war. The formidable tribal chiefs standing solemnly and stiffly, with one hand raised, are distinguished from their soldiers by cloaks and caps, and often carry long staffs; while among the warrior types are archers, spear bearers and soldiers equipped with swords and daggers. Some of the combats seem to be ritual rather than real: one of the most powerful groups is of a pair of men wrestling, and another represents two warriors facing one another, each with both arms raised, perhaps in a ceremonial greeting. The helmets and swords of these figures are of a type which has little or no parallel outside Sardinia, and thereby provide a good illustration of the degree to which Nuraghic culture remained relatively untouched by the rest of Mediterranean life; the strange horned helmets worn by some of the figures are particularly striking.

Not all the bronzes are concerned with war and warriors. A wide range of animals is represented in a series of statuettes that show the Nuraghic people in more relaxed moods – bulls, cows, stags, goats, birds and even monkeys. The model boats, with their prows decorated with the foreparts of a bull or stag or an antelope, are probably replicas of the funerary ships which carried the bodies to burial.

It is always difficult, if tempting, to deduce much about religious beliefs from evidence like this, but a number of examples of female figures holding either children or dead warriors – a kind of Nuraghic pietà – suggest that the tradition represented earlier by the fertility idols continued, and that a mother goddess was worshiped. A male figure with two pairs of eyes, four arms and two shields may represent a Sardinian god, or perhaps a hero. If barely anything is known about the Nuraghic deities, some of their shrines and sacred places at least can be identified. Water seems to have been particularly venerated, and several wells and springs on the island were covered by sacred buildings, with a roof over the actual water source and a paved courtyard to the side, surrounded by stone benches for the worshipers. In some cases, of course, where the waters have medicinal properties, there is good reason for such veneration: after enough invalids had been "cured" by the deity of the well, it would be natural to raise a second building there, and in places the healing powers of Nuraghic gods have been passed on to Christian saints of later ages, and a chapel has been erected on the site of a Nuraghic shrine.

But these are rare examples of survivals from Nuraghic life. In general the culture of Bronze and Early Iron Age Sardinia is notable for its isolation and unique characteristics, and its subsequent complete disappearance. By contrast Sicily was to move, after the confusion of the Late Bronze Age, into a period of brilliant achievement under Greek and Phoenician occupation, with the newcomers mixing with the native peoples. After its conquest by the Carthaginians and the Roman takeover which followed, Sardinia never again achieved any importance or independence, and the last Nuraghic people took to the wild mountains of the interior, where they may well have continued to live for centuries, for all the Romans cared, in a region which is still among the most inaccessible in the Mediterranean.

Nuraghic Sardinia

The Nuraghic culture of Sardinia spans the centuries from the middle of the second millennium BC to the invasion of the Carthaginians in the 6th century with little evidence of any real break in continuity. The isolation of the island itself, and the inaccessibility of much of the interior to the casual visitor – either in ancient or in modern times – explain this and other aspects of Sardinian life. Removed from the ferment of the mainland, the Nuraghic people could retain their own identity as illustrated in the small bronzes they manufactured, and the *nuraghi* themselves were enlarged over the centuries to become some of the most impressive architectural achievements of the ancient world.

1 Over 6,500 *nuraghi* dominate the wild Sardinian landscape, with its mountains and woods broken by the pasturelands which still play a vital part in the economy of the island.

2 Plan showing the phases of work at Barumini. The tower in the center was originally about 17 m high, and probably dates to the earliest period of construction; the four outer towers were added in the early 8th century around it. Less than a century later the outer wall of this structure was reinforced, and an outer line of defense constructed: a series of new towers was built to encircle the central core of the *nuraghe*, and a wall was added which connected them to a couple of free-standing towers from the earlier period. Throughout these phases private houses continued to be constructed outside the walls: many of these remained occupied until Roman times. After Lilliu.

3 Map of Sardinia.

4 The majority of the *nuraghi* are built on immense platforms constructed of huge stone blocks, often unfaced. The towers themselves consist of a series of courses of diminishing diameters, producing a gradual tapering, and a corbeled roof was added. No mortar was used.

5 An air view of the *nuraghe* of Su Nuraxi at Barumini, one of the largest and most complex. The earliest phase of occupation has been dated by Carbon 14 analysis to 1470 ± 200 years. Throughout the succeeding centuries it underwent a series of enlargements and modifications, until it was sacked by the Carthaginians at the end of the 6th century BC.

I

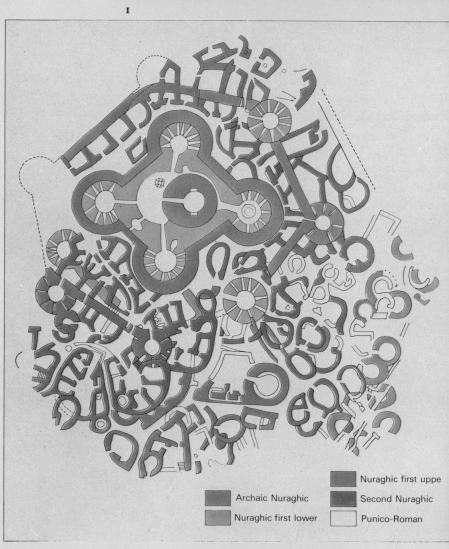

Archaic Nuraghic

Nuraghic first lower

Nuraghic first uppe

Second Nuraghic

Punico-Roman

2

3

5

4

6

6 The Nuraghic bronze figurines, which were produced mainly between the 8th and 6th centuries, combine austerity of style with an amazingly powerful expressivity. Many of the figurines represent warriors, armed generally with spears or bows; the archers often have their quivers slung over their shoulders. In this example the heavy skirt may represent a form of protective armor, consisting of leather studded with bronze; it stands c. 18 cm high. Museo Archeologico Nazionale, Cagliari.

7 Pair of wrestlers. Height 10 cm, length 15·5 cm. The men do not seem to be armed, and the combat is perhaps a ritual one – unless the occasion is a sporting one, a rare moment of relaxation for these austere warriors. Museo Archeologico Nazionale, Cagliari.

8 Nuraghic chieftain, height 20·4 cm. The wide-brimmed hat may be a symbol of his rank, and is reminiscent of similar hats worn by important figures in situla art. Unlike the round helmet of the Warrior of Capestrano, which was probably metal, this hat, together with the cape, was probably made of leather. Nationalmuseet, Copenhagen.

9 Warrior with sword and knotted club of a type still carried by Sardinian shepherds. His cape, like that of the chieftain, is probably a symbol of authority. Museo Archeologico Nazionale, Cagliari.

10 The more fantastic examples, like this warrior with two pairs of eyes, two pairs of arms and two shields, may represent deities or perhaps local heroes. He stands 19 cm high, and comes from the sanctuary of Abini. Museo Archeologico Nazionale, Cagliari.

11 Mother and child (?). Height 11 cm. The smaller figure seems either asleep or dead, and might perhaps be the body of a warrior killed in battle. The mother has her right hand raised in prayer or benediction; she wears a leather cloak around her shoulders. The austerity of expression gives the work an intensity that seems to prefigure the theme of the pietà which was to appear in Italian art centuries later; at the same time the concept of mother goddess is perhaps related to the fertility idols of the Early Bronze Age. Museo Archeologico Nazionale, Cagliari.

12 Bronze boats of this type have also been found on the mainland, both in northern Italy and at Etruscan sites, including Tarquinia and Vetulonia. The prow is decorated with an animal head, and other animal forms can be seen around the sides of the central "cabin" area. The boats may have served as lamps. Museo Archeologico Nazionale, Cagliari.

7

8

9

10

11

12

2 THE DISCOVERY OF EARLY ITALY

The Emperor Claudius, who reigned from 41 to 54 AD, was one of the few Romans to make a serious study of Etruscan culture. This fine cameo is from the Royal Collection at Windsor.

The story of the rediscovery of the past is always intimately bound up with the past itself. Often it seems concerned primarily with sensational finds which by their richness open up whole new vistas, and which themselves create history. The opening of the tomb of Tutankhamun, the excavation of Pompeii, the finding of the palace of Minos at Knossos – these themselves have become historical events, and the acts of discovery have almost equaled in importance the things discovered. By them the past seems to be revealed by a series of great leaps forward.

But the truth, of course, is very different. Only by an immensely slow and painstaking process of search and study can we hope to reconstruct and understand the achievement of past cultures, and only by always remembering that at the very best our information is fragmentary. However much new evidence is found, it represents only the merest fraction of a culture long dead, and we must always remember that the way in which we interpret it is itself always conditioned by our own age and its ways. To think more positively, the understanding of the past presents a constant challenge, and one that can often be stimulated by a study of how our predecessors faced the same questions. Certainly in the case of pre-Roman Italy the understanding of its cultures has been a long process, and is still far from complete.

Antiquarianism in antiquity. Although most of what we now know about Italy before the Romans is the result of the discoveries and research of the last 100 years, by the 15th century the renewed interest in ancient Rome and its history which was to develop during the Renaissance had begun to involve travelers and scholars in a study of Rome's ancestors; and even earlier the first people to show scholarly interest in the Etruscans and others were – not surprisingly, it might seem – the Romans themselves.

Unfortunately, however, the Classical world was not notable for its antiquarian zeal: curiosity about the past, especially the remote past, is essentially a modern phenomenon, and neither Greeks nor Romans were over-concerned to preserve their own ancient monuments or devote to their own origins that spirit of scientific inquiry with which they pursued theories of aesthetics, politics or law. Even that most analytical of ancient historians, Thucydides, was unable to provide more than an extremely brief and confused account of the beginnings of Greek history, while Herodotus' story of the arrival in Italy of the Etruscans creates problems of chronology which still remain unresolved, as we shall see in a later chapter. Nor was much respect shown for material remains: Augustus' proud boast in his will that he had found Rome a city of brick and left it a city of marble would do credit to a modern property developer, and his immense building projects caused the destruction of most of the buildings in Rome.

The Romans' interest in their past was generally the result, therefore, of motives other than disinterested curiosity. Since Rome's power had been acquired at the expense of her Italian neighbors, it was in her interests to emphasize and even exaggerate the strength of her rivals in order to stress the magnitude of her own victories. When Livy describes the wealth and power of the Etruscans and their reputation on land and sea, extending from the Alps to Sicily, he adds luster to their conquest by the Romans, while notably exaggerating their sphere of influence. At the same time the interests of propaganda required that even at the risk of inconsistency these inevitable victims of the spread of Roman power be portrayed as deserving to be conquered, and the Etruscans emerge in ancient accounts as effeminate and immoral, lazy, greedy and pleasure-loving. In the *Aeneid* it takes an intervention from Jupiter himself to make the Etruscans fight. Inspired by the father of gods and men, their leader Tarchon reproaches them for their lethargy: "What are you scared of, Etruscans, cowards that you are? Always idle, why do you carry swords if you do not use them? You are not lazy when it comes to love and struggles in bed, or dancing to the curved flute of Bacchus. Keep your energy for the banquet, then, the loaded tables, the wine cups – those are what you care about." The Etruscans' reputation as voluptuaries incidentally does not seem particularly merited. It is true that scenes of banquets, music and dancing occur frequently in the tomb paintings, sometimes, as in the Tomb of Hunting and Fishing, with erotic overtones, but in general Greek art is far more erotic and the Romans were certainly much more interested in pornography. But propaganda has never drawn its strength from its accuracy, and the Etruscans are consistently given a deliberately "bad press." Earlier in the *Aeneid* Virgil provides his hero Aeneas with a particularly bloodthirsty and brutal Etruscan to kill, in the person of Mezentius, famed for his impiety – a fault which even the Romans must have admitted was rare among the Etruscans, that most religious of

Early excavations at Pompeii, from a book by Sir William Hamilton.

peoples, as Livy calls them. Paradoxically enough, at the same time as all of this, many of the oldest and most distinguished Roman families traced their origins to Etruscan forebears, among them Maecenas, the friend and literary adviser of Augustus and patron of Virgil, who claimed descent from the Etruscan kings of Arezzo.

A few works on history and religion were written by Etruscan authors in Etruscan or Latin, but these are all lost, although later Latin writers like Pliny and Seneca sometimes referred to them and clearly borrowed from them. A more frustrating loss is that of a 20-volume history of the Etruscans, written in Greek by the Emperor Claudius, whose first wife, Urganilla, came from a noble Etruscan family and may have provided him with access to Etruscan sources and archives, if not with a knowledge of the

The Rape of the Sabine Women, here seen in the version of the Baroque painter Pietro da Cortona (1596–1669), was a popular subject throughout the Renaissance and Baroque periods, with its vivid contrast between the violence of the Roman soldiers and the protesting, tearful Sabine victims. Palazzo dei Conservatori, Rome.

Etruscan language. The work was probably scholarly enough, since Claudius had shown academic leanings from an early age. While still a young man he had begun, with the encouragement of Livy, a history of Rome, parts of which he planned to read in public. At the beginning of the reading, however, an immensely fat man arriving late sat down on a bench which collapsed under his weight, causing great amusement among the audience. Even after silence had been restored, Claudius himself continued to break into laughter throughout the reading whenever he remembered the incident. His Etruscan history was also read aloud, although not by the emperor himself: during his reign, when a new wing was added to the Museum of Alexandria at his expense, annual readings of his work by teams of professional readers were held there. In view of Claudius' interest in grammar and language (he added three new letters to the Latin alphabet) the loss of his comments on Etruscan grammar is particularly sad.

But it must be confessed that Claudius' serious and responsible approach to the study of a culture from which Rome had derived so much was exceptional. To some extent the Romans' apparent lack of interest in their predecessors and neighbors in Italy was the result of the immense impact made upon Roman culture by the Greeks: superficially, at least, Roman art, mythology and religion were far more inspired by Greek ideas than by Etruscan or Samnite. It was to the Greeks that they looked for cultural inspiration, and the educated Roman spoke Greek in much the same way as his equivalent in 19th-century Russia spoke French. The nature of the Romans' relationship with the Italic peoples is perhaps best summed up by the traditional account of the rape of the Sabines – an episode from the early days of Rome which proved popular with Renaissance and Baroque artists. According to the story, Romulus, the founder of Rome, realizing that he and his men did not have enough women available to serve as mothers of the future Roman race, invited a group of neighboring Sabines to the festival of the games of the Consualia. At a given signal the Romans drove off the men and seized the Sabine virgins to remedy the deficiency. The story is revealing in a number of ways, however, and not only because of its unselfconscious revelation of much about the Roman character. Within the all-important unit of the family, after all, wives and mothers have played through the centuries an immense part in the formation of the Italian way of life, and even though in public Rome seemed culturally tied to Greece and the east, there remained deep down a residual debt to the Italic peoples, no less important for being unacknowledged, which we shall look at in detail in the last chapter.

The Renaissance. Although in general the Renaissance marks the first serious modern interest in Classical antiquity, that interest, it must be remembered, was highly selective. Rome itself formed the principal subject of inquiry and study, and although, as we shall see, the discovery of Etruscan works of art led to some curiosity about the other ancient cultures of Italy, it was not until the 18th century that any serious research or excavations were conducted. Until then scholars were forced to rely for the most part upon information drawn from Classical writers, which as we have seen was frequently unreliable, and chance finds which were difficult to interpret. Even when at the beginning of the 18th century men of learning began to test their theories by practical excavation, they were hampered and misled by the contributions of writers of the early Renaissance who, inspired by the reviving interest in the past, had produced works on the Etruscans and others which were notable for their imagination and local patriotism rather than accuracy. Among the strangest of the first writers on the Etruscans was a Dominican monk, Fra Giovanni Nanni, generally known as Annio of Viterbo, after the city where he was born and lived from 1432 to 1502, an author who was described by George Dennis, a later and immeasurably greater student of the Etruscans, as "foremost in impudence, unrivalled in voluminous perseverance, a wholesale and crafty forger." Annio knew enough to believe that if he could prove an Etruscan rather than Roman origin for Viterbo, he would advance his city's claims to antiquity and importance. In general such claims can be tested by studying the material remains of a city and excavating for new finds, but this is an expensive and time-consuming method – or at least would have been for Annio. An alternative method, popular in the Renaissance and still useful sometimes today, was to comb ancient literature to find references which might support such a theory. Annio, however, was not content to try only to establish Viterbo as the capital of the Etruscans and leader of the league of 12 Etruscan cities, in itself an absurd claim, but wanted to give it in addition a history so venerable that it could be traced back to before the foundation of Troy; and he was therefore driven, in the absence of the slightest evidence either in the ancient writers or in the material remains to this effect, to forge both. He concocted a number of passages which he then "attributed" to authors such as Archilochus, Xenophon and Cato, and forged several inscriptions in support of them, including two marble tablets which were for a long time regarded as genuine. The absurdity of both Annio's claims and his methods makes them hardly worth discussing, but they served, unfortunately, to confuse a number of later scholars. If they illustrate anything, it is that there is no substitute in archaeological research for scientifically controlled excavations, but these were not to be organized for another 200 years.

At the same time as Annio was faking an Etruscan pedigree for his native city, the discovery of Etruscan works of art was beginning to make an impression on Renaissance artists. In many cases the influence is generalized rather than specific, but sculptors and painters could not fail to respond to the tomb frescoes and statues that, often by the merest chance, were being discovered both in Tuscany and near Rome. The striking resemblance between the so-called Malavolta head, found at Veii and now in the Villa Giulia, and Donatello's Saint George has often been pointed out, although we must remember that Donatello could never have seen the head from Veii, which was discovered centuries after his death. On the other hand he was plainly influenced by works of the same spirit which he had seen, just as Michelangelo must have seen portrayals of winged demons of the kind best represented for us by those on an urn from the tomb of the Volumni near Perugia. We shall probably never be able to trace the exact sources of these influences on Renaissance artists, but it is significant that many of them actually collected antiquities: as early as the beginning of the 15th century Lorenzo Ghiberti had formed a collection of gems and statues, and the Medici rulers of Florence, the patrons and friends of many painters and sculptors, were themselves interested in ancient works of art. By his death in 1492 Lorenzo the Magnificent had amassed the richest collection in Italy, part of which may have found its way down to Rome during the Medici papacies of the following century, and the Grand Dukes of Tuscany continued the tradition. Renaissance artists were therefore in constant

Above: urns in the Tomb of the Volumni, near Perugia. The tomb and its contents date to the second half of the 2nd century BC. The urns are made of travertine, plastered and painted, and the central one, of the master of the family, is richly decorated.

Opposite below: The so-called Malavolta head comes from the Portonaccio sanctuary at Veii, and is named for its excavator. It dates to the second half of the 5th century BC and is 20 cm in height: stylistically it is influenced by contemporary Greek sculpture, especially the work of Polycleitus. The similarity between the head and that of Donatello's St George (*opposite above*) has often been remarked upon, although Donatello's statue was finished in 1417, centuries before the head was discovered. The resemblance is presumably due to a common interest in Classical models. Villa Giulia, Rome, and Bargello, Florence.

Left: Copy of the Hellenistic group of Laocoön and his two sons made by Baccio Bandinelli between 1520 and 1525 for Francis I. His version of the statue is closer to Virgil's description of Laocoön in the *Aeneid*, Book Two, than Montorsoli's slightly later (and better-known) restoration. It is now in the Uffizi, Florence.

Above right: The famous bronze Chimaera was found at Arezzo in the 16th century, and is now in the Museo Archeologico, Florence. It dates to the latter part of the 5th century BC, and stands 80 cm high. The lower parts of the front and back left legs were restored in the Renaissance, perhaps by Cellini, and the tail is a clumsy and inaccurate 19th-century restoration.

Above: Johannes Winckelmann (1717–68), sometimes known as the Father of Archaeology, whose systematic study of the remains of Classical antiquity available to him provided a foundation for the work of later scholars.

contact with ancient masterpieces, and both studied and copied them. Michelangelo was among those consulted on how the famous Hellenistic statue of Laocoön and his sons should be restored, and Baccio Bandinelli, his rival, was commissioned by Cardinal Giulio de Medici, later Pope Clement VII, to make a copy of it to present to Francis I, king of France, although on its completion Clement liked the copy too much to part with it, and sent it instead to Florence where it was placed in the courtyard of the Medici Palace. As additional works were discovered their influence spread: in the middle of the 16th century a number of important Etruscan bronzes came to light, including the famous Arringatore (or Orator) found on the shores of Lake Trasimene and the Chimaera from Arezzo, which was repaired by Benvenuto Cellini.

But in spite of the excitement produced by these masterpieces, there was no serious attempt to study them systematically. The first man to try to collect and evaluate all known information on ancient Tuscany was the Scots scholar Sir Thomas Dempster, who between 1616 and 1625 compiled seven volumes, based for the most part on ancient sources and called *De Etruria Regali*. Dempster was a Scottish Catholic who had taught at the University of Pisa in the time of Galileo, and had used all the information on the Etruscans that he could find in order to demonstrate that it was they and not the Romans who were the true founders of Italian civilization. His work was not published for over 100 years, however, and it appeared finally in Florence in 1723 when it was rediscovered and shown to a visiting English nobleman, Thomas Coke, later to become the Earl of Leicester. Coke arranged to subsidize its publication, with a commentary by Filippo Buonarotti.

18th-century initiatives. It was, of course, not by mere chance that interest in ancient Italy was growing in these years. The beginning of the 18th century was marked by renewed cultural and political activity in the provincial centers of Tuscany, and cities like Arezzo, Volterra and Cortona were anxious to prove themselves the equals of Florence. Now Dempster's theories provided them with grounds for superiority, since Florence was by general agreement a city of Roman foundation, while their origins were

Etruscan. To confirm this glorious past, in 1728 excavations were begun at Volterra, which provided material for the foundation of a museum there, named for its founder, the Abbe Mario Guarnacci, which is still one of the finest and best-displayed collections in Italy. In 1726 an Etruscan Academy was established at the Tuscan hilltop town of Cortona, devoted to the study of Etruscan art and history with a president known as the *lucumone* (the Etruscan word for ruler or prince).

In some cases these new initiatives produced only an unorganized hunt for antiquities, the price of which naturally soared, and theories that were not much more credible than Annio's. The Etruscan language, which seems always to have attracted the more imaginative of scholars, was responsible for many of these: one researcher identified it as the language spoken on Noah's Ark, while the secretary of the French Académie des Inscriptions claimed that it was Gallic in origin. But at the same time other scholars were making serious and valuable contributions to the development of Etruscology, including Anton Francesco Gori who produced catalogs to the Cortona and Volterra museums.

The confusion was not only caused by the excesses of local patriotism. From the beginning of the study of pre-Roman art, the problem of Greek influence created a stumbling block, not only because many Etruscan sculptures and paintings make use of Greek themes and styles, including, for example, the engraved bronze cist found at Palestrina in 1738 by Francesco Ficoroni, but because large quantities of Greek vases were found together with the Etruscan objects in the tombs. For a long time these Greek vases were believed to be Etruscan, and it was only in 1806 that Luigi Lanzi published a work entitled *De' vasi antichi dipinti volgarmente chiamati etruschi*, which tried to establish scientific criteria for distinguishing between Etruscan and Greek pottery. Lanzi is the first great name in the history of Etruscology, and he wrote works not only dealing with art and history, but also a study of the Etruscan language. He certainly provides a much more perceptive analysis of the Etruscans than Johannes Winckelmann, his much more famous contemporary, who inevitably compared the Etruscans, to their detriment, with the Greeks. Winckelmann's taste for the "noble simplicity and calm grandeur" of Greek art – or at least those examples of Greek art available to him – led him to condemn those aspects of Etruscan art which did not conform to this (he must have found the Chimaera of Arezzo particularly repugnant) and to attribute the other characteristics to the universality of Greek art. He even used the more violent and melancholy aspects of Etruscan art as a stick with which to beat their Renaissance successors, condemning artists like Michelangelo and Daniele da Volterra for falling under their influence: according to Winckelmann, "he who has seen one of Michelangelo's drawings has seen them all." On the other hand, Winckelmann was one of the first scholars to realize that there existed other cultures in ancient Italy besides the Romans and Etruscans, and although he had little to say about Oscan or Samnite art, he at least acknowledged their existence.

The tombs of Tarquinia and Cerveteri. The question of the "originality" of Etruscan art, and the extent of its debt to Greece, continued to obsess 18th-century writers and artists. In his campaign to demonstrate the Italian rather than Greek origins of Roman art, the great engraver Gian Battista Piranesi produced a number of engravings of Etruscan architectural remains and reconstructions of Etruscan temples,

"The Orator," bronze statue 1·8 m high, found at Sanguineto on Lake Trasimene. It was made around 100 BC, and is a portrait of a local magistrate called Aulus Metellus, whose name appears in an Etruscan inscription on the hem of the toga. The realism of the face and the vividness of gesture seem to foreshadow the naturalism of later Roman portraits. Museo Archeologico, Florence.

The Ficoroni cist from Praeneste, mid-4th century BC. The body of the cylindrical container, which was used for holding toilet articles, is richly engraved with scenes drawn from the story of the Argonauts. The artist has superbly conveyed the sense of depth and perspective by a masterly command of foreshortening. The lid is decorated with a group representing Dionysus and two satyrs, which also serves as a handle. The whole piece is 75 cm high. Villa Giulia, Rome.

inevitably more beautiful than accurate. The controversy is far from dead, and the precise nature of the relationships between Greek, Etruscan and Roman culture is still highly debatable, but by the beginning of the 19th century at least more evidence was becoming available. In the course of only a few years a series of major discoveries was made, often by chance. Between 1827 and 1834 eight painted tombs were found at Tarquinia, including one of the most famous of all, the Tomb of the Triclinium. A description of the tomb is provided by George Dennis, the English amateur (in the best sense of the word) whose book, *Cities and Cemeteries of Etruria*, was first published in 1848 and not only still provides an incomparably vivid description of the Etruscan sites and sights he visited, but has preserved for us a description of much material that was subsequently lost:

"The first peep within this tomb is startling, especially if the sun's rays happen at the moment to enter the chamber, which they do in the course of the afternoon. Such a blaze of rich colour on the walls and roof, and such life in the figures that dance around! In truth, the excellent state of preservation – the wonderful brilliancy of the colours, almost as fresh after three or four and twenty centuries, as when first laid on – the richness of the costumes – the strangeness of the attitudes – the spirit, the vivacity, the joyousness of the whole scene – the decidedly Etruscan character of the design, distinct from the Greek and yet in certain points approximating to it – render this one of the most interesting tombs yet opened in Etruria . . . The broad beam of the ceiling is painted with ivy leaves and berries; the slopes are chequered with black, red, blue, yellow, and white. Where the painting has suffered, it is not so much from the colours fading, as in the Querciola tomb, as from the stucco peeling from the wall, and from streams of a semi-transparent deposit from the rock itself, which has obliterated a considerable portion of the banquet; but there still remain, little impaired, two figures of opposite sexes, reclining on a couch, attended by a female servant with an *alabastos*, or pot of ointment, and a boy with a wine-jug, while a *subulo* stands in one corner playing the double-pipes. The man on the second couch is almost obliterated; and of the single male figure on the third couch, hardly a fragment is now to be traced. The sex of the figures is distinguishable by the colour; that of the men is a deep red; that of the women, being left unpainted, is of the ground-colour of the wall – a rich creamy white . . . It is worthy of remark that all the women in this tomb, even the slave who is waiting on the banqueters, are decently robed. So it is in the other tombs; and this tends to belie the charge brought against the Etruscans by the Greeks, that the men were waited on by naked handmaids. No such representation has been found on any Etruscan painting or relief yet discovered; on the contrary, the women are draped with more than Greek modesty. Only in one tomb in this necropolis, that of the Scrofa Nera, is a woman depicted with bosom bare. The Etruscans may not have been better than their neighbours in such matters, but any reproach of this sort comes from the Greeks with a very bad grace . . . The colours in this tomb are black, deep red, or maroon, light red, blue, and yellow. In few of the painted tombs in this necropolis do we meet with green. All the colours, except the blue which in the leaves of the trees has much faded, retain their original brilliancy; and it must be remembered that three or four-and-twenty centuries have elapsed since they were laid on, and that they are on the bare rock, the natural creamy hue of which forms the ground to the whole. Damp does not seem here to have affected them as in some other tombs (Ruspi maintains that the damp has been a preservative of the colours. He remarks, that when the sun enters this tomb, and dries the surface of the wall, the figures in that part appear more natural and beautiful than the rest, because they then lose their extreme depth of colour, and acquire just the tint the ancient artist intended)."

Unfortunately the enthusiasm and perception of the first discoverers of the tombs were not accompanied by any knowledge of how best to preserve them. We now know that in order to save the tomb paintings it is necessary to maintain a constant temperature and to avoid precisely that strong light which Dennis admired, and the effects of which he described without realizing their consequences. The colors of the frescoes in the Tomb of the Triclinium are now far from brilliant, and a few years ago they were stripped from the walls of the tomb in the Etruscan cemetery and transferred to canvas, and are now on display, looking very faded, in the Tarquinia Museum. On the other hand, it is hardly fair to blame the early enthusiasts for not using skills and knowledge which they did not possess, and at least in the Tomb of the Triclinium damage was kept to a minimum. Elsewhere more harm was done. The Tomb of Orcus, one of the largest and most complex of those at Tarquinia, was discovered in 1868 by a French army officer, quartered in Rome, who, in his attempt to remove some of the frescoes and carry them back to Paris, destroyed many of them and defaced others, with the result that large areas of the walls show only blank rough rock surfaces. In spite of such losses, however, both accidental and

Tomb of the Reliefs in the necropolis of Banditaccia, Cerveteri. Carved in the late 4th or early 3rd century BC, it is composed of a single underground chamber, decorated in stucco with relief representations of military articles and objects from daily life. Notice, for example, the various implements (long-bladed knife, ax etc.) on the left pillar. An inscription identifies the tomb as the vault of the Matuna family.

Cerveteri, necropolis of Banditaccia: view along one of the streets of tombs. The street was carved out of the soft volcanic rock known as tufa, and the tracks worn in it by the wheels of the funeral carriages can still be seen. This section of the necropolis was probably constructed in the late 6th century BC.

deliberate, the general mass of new material discovered during this period probably fared better than discoveries made elsewhere in Italy during the previous century and even later. Although the excavation of such sites as Vulci and Cerveteri was certainly no model of scientific precision, at least they suffered less than Pompeii and Herculaneum, where so much was willfully destroyed or stolen. And it is easy for us to be hypocritical in our condemnation of past follies. We read with horror of a Pompeian guide who told a 19th-century visitor to the excavations to have a good look round: "Let me know if there is anything you like. I can steal it for you when there is a full moon." But even today neither tomb robbers nor their customers are unknown at Etruscan sites.

Meanwhile the discoveries continued. In 1836 the Regolini Galassi tomb was opened at Cerveteri, with its stupendous collection of goldwork, fortunately immediately transferred to the Museo Etrusco Gregoriano in Rome, where it forms part of the Vatican collections. A few years earlier it had been the turn of Vulci to provide sensational discoveries.

"The wide, wide moor, a drear, melancholy waste, stretches around you, no human being seen on its expanse; the dark, lonely castle rises in the midst, with the majestic bridge spanning the abyss at its side; the Fiora frets in its rocky bed far beneath your feet, and its murmurs conveyed to your ear by the tall cliffs you stand on, are the sole disturbers of the solemn stillness. Deep is the dreariness of that moor . . . The scene is replete with matter for melancholy reflection, deepened by the sense that the demon of malaria has here set up his throne, and rendered this once densely-peopled spot 'a land accurst.' In the early part of 1828 some oxen were ploughing near the castle, when the ground suddenly gave way beneath them, and disclosed an Etruscan tomb with two broken vases. This led to further research, which was at first carried on unknown to the Prince of Canino, but at the close of the year he took the excavations into his own hands, and in the course of four months he brought to light more than two thousand objects of Etruscan antiquity, and all from a plot of ground of three or four acres. Other excavators soon came into the field; every one who had land in the neighbourhood tilled it for this novel harvest, and all with abundant success; the Feoli, Candelori, Campanari, Fossati, – all enriched themselves and the Museums of Europe with treasures from this sepulchral mine. Since that time the Prince or his widow has annually excavated on this site, and never in vain . . ."

These examples represent only a fraction of the finds which continued to be made throughout the 19th century. At Chiusi, Vetulonia, Perugia, Orvieto, Veii, Marzabotto, Bologna, and throughout Tuscany and Latium tombs and buildings were uncovered, with ever-increasing care to recover them and their contents in as complete a state as possible, and to study them in a systematic way. Some of the finds, however, remained in private hands. Dennis records a visit to the house of the three Campanari brothers in Tuscania, who between them combined the excavation, study and sale of antiquities.

"Besides their society, which rendered Toscanella at that period a place of much interest to the antiquary, these gentlemen had many things rich and rare, the produce of their *scavi*, to offer to the traveller's notice. Their house was a museum of Etruscan antiquities. In the vestibule were stone sarcophagi with figures reclining on the lids; and sundry bas-reliefs in *terracotta* were embedded in the walls. Their garden was a most singular place. You seemed transported to some scene of Arabian romance, where the people were all turned to stone, or lay spell-bound, awaiting the touch of a magician's wand to restore them to life and activity. All round the garden, under the close-embowering shade of trellised vines, beneath the drooping boughs of the weeping willow, the rosy bloom of the oleander, or the golden fruit of the orange and citron, lay Lucumones of aristocratic dignity – portly matrons, bedecked with jewels – stout youths, and graceful maidens – reclining on the lids of their coffins, or rather on their festive couches – meeting with fixed stare the astonishment of the stranger, yet with a distinct individuality of feature and expression, and so life-like withal, that, 'like Pygmalion's statue waking,' each seemed to be on the point of warming into existence. Lions, sphinxes, and chimaeras dire, in stone, stood among them, as guardians of the place; and many a figure of quaint character, and petrified life, looked down on you from the vine-shaded terraces, high above the walls of the garden."

The first collections. The immense amount of new material required organizing, and the new kingdom of Italy created a Department of Antiquities responsible for supervising and undertaking excavations and publishing finds. The official bulletin of excavations in Italy, *Notizie degli Scavi*, first appeared in 1876 and still appears annually as a major source of information on new discoveries. The objects themselves required homes, and many new museums were created, while old ones were enlarged. The Vatican's Etruscan collection had been inaugurated in 1836, with the material from the Regolini Galassi tomb. New museums were formed at Tarquinia, Chiusi and other Etruscan centers, and in 1870 the Archaeological Museum of Florence was set up. The Medici collections, enriched by the additions made by the Grand Dukes of Tuscany throughout the 16th and 17th centuries, had passed into the Uffizi Gallery in 1737 along with the paintings in accordance with the wishes of the last of the Medici, Anna Maria Lodovica. Now, with the increasing interest in

The Warrior of Capestrano, 6th century BC, Museo Nazionale, Chieti. Height 209 cm. The discovery of this impressive statue, perhaps a grave marker, in 1934 served to confirm the existence of a native sculptural tradition in Italy, comparatively unaffected by Greek and Orientalizing influences. It is discussed further in Chapter 4.

antiquities, a new home was found for them and new finds added. In some cases pieces which had originally been in private hands passed into public collections – not always with their owner's approval. In 1857 the governor of the Roman bank of the Monte di Pietà discovered that the bank's director, the Marchese Gianpietro Campana, had withdrawn three million *scudi* from the bank's funds without permission. Campana was sent to prison and his immensely valuable private collection of antiquities was confiscated and sold. Although some of the objects ended up in Russia and France, many were bought by the Archaeological Museum of Florence, where vases from the Campana collection can now be seen. The most famous vase in Florence, the François vase of Greek origin, found in an Etruscan tomb near Chiusi, entered the museum by a more orthodox route when it was bought by the Tuscan authorities for 1,000 *scudi*, but few pieces can have had so disturbed a subsequent career. Found in fragments, it was restored and placed on display in the Archaeological Museum. In 1900 the museum guard on duty in the room where the François vase was displayed, in a sudden and apparently unexplained fit of fury, picked up a chair and smashed the vase to pieces. In the ensuing confusion one of the visitors to the museum walked off with one of the fragments, so that when the vase was re-restored, it was lacking a piece. Some years later, however, the missing piece was returned, apparently in remorse, by the heirs of its taker after his death. A few years ago it was decided to take the vase to pieces yet again, this time in the interests of scholarship, and to reinsert the recovered piece, although the more immediate cause of this new restoration was the damage caused to the vase by the vibrations of traffic outside the museum and the footsteps of visitors within. In addition the sunlight to which the vase had been exposed in its display case had begun to harm the painting on it; like Dennis and his fellow explorers, more recent museum directors had been unaware of the damage that natural light can do. When the restorers began work, they found that several sections had been overenthusiastically repaired and repainted by their 19th-century predecessors. These were removed and the vase was put together, it is to be hoped for the last time, and is once again on display in the Archaeological Museum.

The greatest of all collections of pre-Roman art from Italy was inaugurated in Rome in 1889, when the Villa Giulia, constructed for Pope Julius III in the 16th century, was converted into a museum devoted to Etruscan, Faliscan, Umbrian and Sabine art, and the excavations of the following years immensely enriched its holdings. The contents of the Etruscan Barberini and Bernardini tombs uncovered at Palestrina, and the famous terracotta statues found at Veii in 1916, are just some of its treasures, and as a result of modernization and remodeling which took place there between 1955 and 1960 the Villa Giulia has become an all-too-rare example of the intelligent display of magnificent objects.

The discovery of other cultures. By the middle of the 19th century the Etruscans were clearly established as a people whose culture merited serious attention and study, but relatively little attention had been paid to the other peoples of ancient Italy. The first scientific evidence of the existence of an Italic people who predated the Etruscans came in 1853, when Count Gozzadini excavated an Early Iron Age cemetery at the village of Villanova, and his finds stimulated a fresh burst of exploration. The discovery of an even earlier culture, that of the Bronze Age Terramara people of Emilia, was described in a work by Gastaldi published in 1862,

Nuovi cenni sugli oggetti di alta antichità dell' Italia; and in northeastern Italy, in the Veneto, A. Prosdocimi, the director of the museum at Este, excavated a series of tombs and in 1882 published a proposed chronology of Este culture which, with minor modifications, still holds good today. We shall be looking at all three of these cultures – the Villanovan, Terramara and Este – in the next chapter, where we shall also meet the leading Italian figure in prehistoric studies at the end of the 19th century, Luigi Pigorini. Many of Pigorini's theories have now been abandoned, and some modern scholars are inclined to dismiss much of his work, but if new finds have in general served to disprove much that he believed, his contribution to the development of a serious interest in Italian prehistory was immense, and finds a worthy memorial in Rome's Museum of Prehistory which has been named for him. As a result of the work of Pigorini and others, scholars became increasingly aware that neither Etruscans nor Romans could be

The François vase, made and painted in Athens around 570 BC by Ergotimos and Kleitias. It is decorated with numerous mythological scenes, involving over 200 figures, most of whom were labeled with their names. It was probably exported to Chiusi as a "collector's piece," and was found there in the necropolis of Fonte Rotella, in the 19th century; it is now in the Museo Archeologico, Florence. Height c. 72 cm.

understood without a knowledge of their predecessors, and in 1910 Angelo Mosso in his book *The Dawn of Mediterranean Civilisation* was able to write the following:

"The most serious lacuna of modern archaeology is in connection with the origin of the Etruscans and the time preceding the foundation of Rome, and these are just the most vital points in our history. Professor Boni discovered upon the virgin soil in the Roman Forum the tomb of a child, prepared by his parents with an affectionate care that fills us with admiration. The body was enclosed in the hollowed-out trunk of an oak-tree, which was placed in a small chapel built of pieces of tufa. Upon the child's body was a copper belt with clasp and pendant. On the right arm was an ivory bracelet; there were spiral rings, too, made of copper wire, and a large number of glass and enamel beads were attached to the tunic; but most interesting of all are several fibulae of bronze with disks of amber.

"This interment is little earlier than the eighth century. During the iron age, upon the hills round the Forum, lived a rich and highly civilised people, but we know little or nothing of the primitive Romans, and the case is the same with regard to the Etruscans."

In general it has been our century that has discovered the other cultures of ancient Italy, and the discoveries are inevitably incomplete. Although, as we shall see, much is now known about the Etruscans, other peoples remain much more mysterious – the Ligurians, for example, or the Picenes – and the relationships between the various Italic tribes are often puzzling. Nor are all new finds the result of planned excavations: the chance discovery in

"The Temples at Paestum," drawn by W. Brockedon, from a sketch by Captain Sir George Back. Engraved by R. Brandard.

1934 of the statue known as the Warrior of Capestrano in eastern Italy totally changed the study of Italic sculpture, not only by providing a major new example, but by prompting a reassessment of earlier finds. In the past anything that was not Greek or Roman had been labeled as Etruscan. It is now clear that other cultures were producing works of art in their own style, related to but by no means entirely dependent on Etruscan models; as a result, pieces like the Mars of Todi (discussed in Chapter 4) are being looked at in a new way, and no longer simply labeled as Etruscan. Nonetheless there is always a tendency to relate new finds to familiar cultures. In the summer of 1968 archaeologists excavating in an area outside the walls of Paestum in southern Italy found a group of tombs with painted sides and lids. We shall be looking at the paintings in a later chapter, since they form a rare and precious collection of Italic art and were, with one exception, produced at a time when Paestum was a Samnite city; only the Tomb of the Diver dates to the Greek period there. The finders of the tombs, therefore, urged on by massive press and television coverage, immediately hailed the paintings in the Tomb of the Diver as Greek, which would indeed have been an exciting discovery, since few traces survive of Greek mural or easel paintings either in Greece or in Italy. Now that the immediate excitement has died down, however, it seems far more probable that the paintings are the work of a local artist who was strongly influenced by contemporary Greek pottery styles, although he was equally aware of developments in Etruscan art. The fact that they are Italic in workmanship does not lessen their value, of course, but it is significant that the

Excavation in progress at the Banditaccia necropolis, Orvieto.

archaeologists responsible for finding them, in their inevitable and easily understandable overreaction to their discovery, should have attributed them to a Greek hand.

The discoveries at Paestum are among the most sensational of the last few years, but there have been many others. Nonetheless there remains a vast difference between the present state of Etruscology and that of the study of early Italic cultures. Our knowledge of the Etruscans, already considerable, has been vastly enlarged by the finds described in a later chapter, many of which have come not only from tombs and cemeteries, but from religious sanctuaries and urban settlements. In the case of the Italic cultures, however, new material is not serving so much to enrich an already existing picture as to provide a starting point for an assessment of their achievements. It has always been thought, for example, that the peoples of eastern Italy, from the provinces now known as Abruzzi and Molise, were among the most backward and underdeveloped in Italy. But a series of excavations begun in 1965 at Campovalano has uncovered about 200 tombs, mostly dating to the 6th century BC, and some with material that goes back as far as the 9th century BC and the dawn of the Iron Age. Far from primitive, the art represented in the graves is rich and sophisticated, and the bronze and iron weapons and vessels and the elaborate pottery are evidence of a high cultural level. Nor did these early Sabellian warriors confine their activities to their own regions: both in Sardinia and in Corsica tombs have recently been found with similar contents, probably the graves of mercenaries who left their own territory to fight abroad.

Around Rome itself new evidence is coming to light about the Romans' predecessors. To the northeast a Sabine cemetery has been excavated at Colle del Forno: the Sabines are mainly known to us from the legends and stories incorporated into Rome's early history, as we saw earlier, and it is interesting to find that these "rude, uncultivated barbarians" had in fact trading and artistic links with the Faliscans, the Etruscans and the cultures of the Adriatic coast. To the south of Rome the widening of a road near Castel di Decima uncovered some tombs of the 8th and 7th centuries BC with gold, silver and amber ornaments and, in four of the tombs, chariots. In all these cases such riches were surprising and in contrast to the literary and historical picture.

Meanwhile in southern Italy the Daunians of northern Apulia are beginning to make their appearance. Known mainly by their characteristic style of pottery, this Early Iron Age Italic culture had its center at Arpi, but a number of other settlements have been found with elaborate defenses, in one case extending for over 8 miles. Although so little is still known about them, the Daunians must have been an important people throughout southern Italy: their pottery is found over a wide area, and their history was obviously a long one. Their sites were first settled in the 8th century BC. A period of disturbances between 700 and 550 BC, during which the Daunian centers were fortified, was followed by a renewed prosperity which lasted until sometime after 400 BC, when they were absorbed by the Samnites.

While the picture of the indigenous cultures of Italy is becoming more and more complex, at the same time more is being learned of the impact on

Above: Air view of the Banditaccia necropolis, Cerveteri. This cemetery lies to the northwest of the city, and was in continuous use from the 7th century to around 100 BC. The circular tumuli are earlier in date than the rectangular cube-tombs, which began to appear in the middle of the 6th century.

Opposite above: Reconstruction of a small Etruscan temple from Alatri in the garden of the Villa Giulia, Rome. The elaborate decoration was of terracotta.

Opposite below: The discovery of a tomb at Tarquinia by a team from the Lerici Foundation, using a periscope.

The elongated bronze statuettes of the Swiss sculptor Alberto Giacometti (1901–66) are clearly influenced by Etruscan bronzes. Here one of his works (*opposite*), "Standing Woman II, 1960," is seen in contrast to the figure of an Etruscan priest (*above*), now in the Villa Giulia, Rome.

Italian civilization of foreign people. Throughout southern Italy and Sicily archaeologists are continuing to explore the Greek cities and colonies and are trying to relate their finds to the Greeks' Italic contemporaries. New discoveries suggest that life in Early Iron Age Italy was much more international than used to be thought. On the island of Ischia, off the coast near Naples, a Greek commercial center of the early 8th century BC has been excavated at Pithecoussae. This Greek settlement, the forerunner of the Greek colony of Cumae on the mainland, seems to have attracted other foreigners: Phoenicians were among the inhabitants, and there were also cultural links with Syria. Nor were these merely transient merchant-traders: an urn of local manufacture has been found, which was used for the burial of a child, with an inscription in Aramaic suggesting that whole families must have moved there from the east. At the same time the colony maintained links with the Etruscans, as is shown by the appearance in the tombs of Tarquinia of scarab seals of a type peculiar in the western Mediterranean to Ischia, and a metal industry which developed on the island put it in contact with the leading Etruscan mining centers.

New methods of exploration. In recent years archaeologists engaged in the excavation of many of these sites have been greatly helped by the development and application of new methods of exploration. The work of the Lerici Foundation in identifying and examining the Etruscan tombs is well known. By taking readings of the degree of conductivity of electricity at a series of points in a particular area using machines known as potentiometers, technicians can establish whether tombs or other structures lie underground. And, once a tomb has been located, a hole can be drilled down through the earth and rock to penetrate the roof of the tomb through which a narrow metal cylinder is lowered, equipped with a miniature camera and flashlight. Photographs are then taken, which show whether the tomb has already been robbed or damaged, and whether the immediate expense of a full-scale excavation is justified.

Photography of a different kind, but equally valuable, is air photography. By his study of the photographs taken by the R.A.F. for military purposes during the last years of World War II, and his own subsequent investigations, John Bradford identified the location of two cemeteries at Cerveteri and over 400 tombs within them. Even more remarkably perhaps, his work in southern Italy revealed the remains of a culture 4,000 years older than the Etruscans': air photographs taken in 1943 of the plain of the Tavoliere in Apulia showed dark circular areas where in spite of the summer heat the crops were less parched. By examining these areas in detail, Bradford was able to find traces of ditches, whose soil had retained their moisture and thereby had produced the dark marks visible in the photographs, and within the ditches traces of clay on the rock surface, indicating where huts had been built. These groups of huts surrounded by a ditch date to the Middle Neolithic period, and almost 300 have now been found. It is probably safe to say that without the air photographs, and Bradford's perception, these Neolithic villages would never have been discovered.

If some archaeological features are visible only from the air, others are by now under water, and the development of new techniques of underwater archaeology has also produced important discoveries. At the sites of the Early Bronze Age lake villages of northern Italy, much valuable material has been recovered from the lakes themselves, and new methods of conservation have made possible the preservation and study of the finds. And a whole new field of study for Etruscologists has been opened up by a series of explorations and excavations along the west coast of Italy, where in the last few years a team led by Professor Anna McCann has been studying the underwater remains of Etruscan ports and harbors, including those at Populonia, Cosa and Pyrgi.

Not all discoveries are made in the field. New laboratory techniques can also produce surprises, even in the study of material already known and studied. We shall see in the next chapter how by cleaning a bronze *tintinnabulum* in the Bologna Museum, scientists were able to throw new light on ancient weaving techniques. And when, after the disastrous flood of 1966, technicians in the Florence Restoration Laboratory were repairing part of a bronze vase found in a 7th-century BC Etruscan tomb, they found on it an inscription in New Babylonian, the only example of its kind ever to have been discovered, which opens up a new perspective on Etruscan relations with the east. The vase entered the museum's collection in 1889, but had it not been for the flood and the damage it caused the inscription would probably never have been found.

And yet in spite of all this progress so many basic questions remain unanswered. The very problems that puzzled Herodotus or Dionysius of Halicarnassus still vex modern scholars, although their approach to them is changing. It will take many years before all the new finds can be absorbed and their significance fully understood – and by then with luck our successors will have a host of new discoveries of their own. It must be confessed that if our methods are somewhat more scientific than those of Annio or Viterbo, the state of our knowledge about the Messapians or the Ligurians is little more advanced than his about the Etruscans, and the very real progress of the last few years only serves to demonstrate how little we still know. Curiously enough, perhaps as a result of their air of mystery, the peoples of early Italy have always seemed to appeal to laymen as well as scholars, and the Etruscomania of the 18th and 19th centuries has been followed in our own time by a comparable interest. D. H. Lawrence's *Etruscan Places* is only the best-known of the tributes to the evocative power of the remains of Etruscan civilization, and the learned if eccentric theories of the *studiosi* of 18th-century Tuscany find their modern successors in the popular handbooks of today that promise to reveal the mysteries and offer more or less ingenious decipherments of the Etruscan language. In the visual arts, too, Etruscan and Italic art has had its effect. Henry Moore is a notable example of a sculptor influenced by the rugged, primitive qualities of Etruscan art, which, according to the British aesthetician Clive Bell, possesses the vital artistic quality of "significant form." The spindly wire figures of Giacometti seem descendants of elongated Etruscan bronze figurines, and Etruscan vividness of characterization can be seen in the portrait busts of Marino Marini.

The field archaeologist and the student of early Italy can only hope that increasing knowledge will inspire yet greater interest in the Etruscans and their contemporaries and will not, by removing at least some of the mystery, disperse the enthusiasm. The Italian 20th-century painter Massimo Campigli, whose work has sometimes been described as Etruscan in inspiration, has said, in rejecting the description, that the term "Etruscan" is nowadays employed for whatever is not properly understood. Let us hope that future generations will not be able to use it in the same way.

Jewelry in Early Italy

For both Etruscans and Greeks gold jewelry provided almost limitless opportunities for virtuosity of technique and imagination. Unlike medieval or Byzantine jewelry, which uses precious and semiprecious stones to enrich a flat surface, these gold pieces have an almost sculptural quality. Their richness is produced by a wide range of ways of working the gold. In addition to modeling and casting, designs could be beaten in relief, incised, applied in the form of filigree work, inlaid or chased. Most elaborate of all was the technique of granulation, employed by the Etruscans, whereby tiny granules of gold were soldered on to a base, either to cover an entire area or to create a pattern.

In the 7th century BC the predominant influence on the production of jewelry throughout Italy was an Orientalizing one. The sumptuous decorations on the finds from Cerveteri and Praeneste represent the effects of eastern styles, either borrowed from the Greeks or resulting from direct contacts with Egypt and Asia. Recent discoveries in Latium, in fact, suggest that in some cases these Orientalizing trends made their way directly into the local cultures, presumably as the result of trade, rather than being introduced by either Etruscans or Greeks.

Although the Greek and Etruscan pieces have much in common, it is probably true to say that Greek goldsmiths generally aimed for delicacy of effect, often by the use of gold leaf, while the Etruscans preferred richness and weightiness, applying heavy encrustations. In either case these pieces were never intended, of course, for daily wear: they represent for the most part finds from tombs, objects worthy to accompany their owners to the next life.

1

2

1 Gold brooch, 6th century BC. Museo Archeologico, Ferrara. The double portrait of Hermes is surrounded by an inner band of granulation and an outer band of small and large droplets.

2 Gold pectoral from the Bernardini Tomb at Praeneste, 7th century BC. Villa Giulia, Rome. The richness of the relief decoration, consisting of small Orientalizing animals, creates an effect of almost barbaric splendor.

3 Gold diadem, 4th century BC. Museo Archeologico, Taranto. The richness of this late Classical piece is further enhanced by enameling and the attachment of small precious stones.

4 Etruscan gold bracelets from Vetulonia, 6th century BC. Museo Archeologico, Florence. The effect of the broad bands is offset by the delicate filigree decoration.

5 Two rings and an earring, 7th–6th century BC. British Museum. The heavy use of granulation, even on pieces as delicate as these, is characteristic of Etruscan work of the period. Compare the similar techniques on the next piece.

6 Gold earring, probably from Vulci, 4th century BC. British Museum. The round center is decorated in relief, and the elements around show a variety of techniques – granulation, small globules and the use of gold leaf.

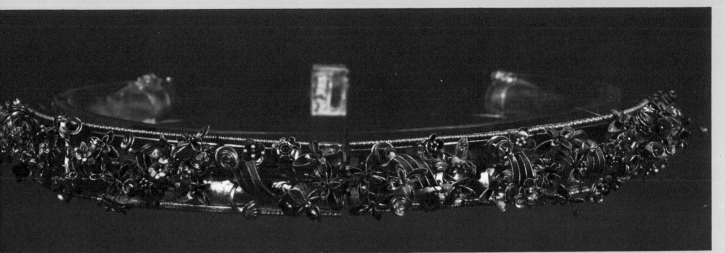

3

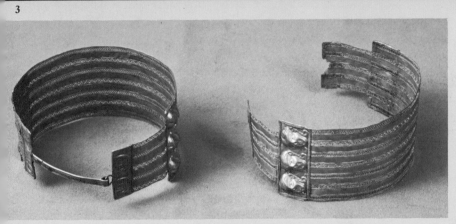

4

5

6

7 Necklace of gold *bullae* (lentil-shaped decorative elements), late 4th or early 3rd century BC. Vatican Museums. The use of *bullae* by Etruscan goldsmiths dates to the end of the 4th century BC: they are frequently embossed with scenes from Greek mythology.

8 The Praeneste Fibula, Museo Pigorini, Rome. This piece has been the subject of considerable discussion. The original claim that it came from the Bernardini Tomb at Praeneste has been challenged a number of times, and attempts have been made to prove it a fake. The importance of the fibula lies in its inscription, which, if genuine, provides valuable information on the state of the Latin language in the early 7th century BC; but even if the fibula itself is ancient, the inscription may have been forged. In any case, as David Ridgway has recently shown, the evidence is so confusing that the truth will probably never be known: in the meantime the piece cannot be regarded as reliable evidence for its period or its alleged archaeological context.

9 Ivy-leaf wreath, c. 300 BC. British Museum. It shows a magnificent use of gold leaf, all the more effective in that it is less elaborate and more restrained than some other examples.

10 Gold earring from Crispiano, 4th–3rd century BC. Museo Archeologico, Taranto. A magnificent piece, which effectively contrasts the mass of the body of the piece with the delicate floral decoration and droplets suspended from fine chains.

11 Ajax falling on his sword, cast of a late 5th-century BC carnelian scarab originally set in a gold ring. Etruscan work. Metropolitan Museum, New York. 1·4 × 2·1 cm.

7

8

9

10

11

3 FROM BRONZE TO IRON IN NORTHERN ITALY

Early Bronze Age bronze dagger from the hoard of metal objects discovered at Castione dei Marchesi in the Po valley. The style of the hilt and the design incised on the blade suggest parallels with contemporary cultures to the north of the Alps

Shortly after 1000 BC the technique of ironworking, which had been discovered and developed by the Hittites in the Near East, spread westward to Europe. Its arrival marked a turning point in western civilization: in a sense, the Iron Age it ushered in was to last until the 19th century and the Industrial Revolution, and in a modified form is still with us today. The Villanovans, the most advanced of Early Iron Age Italic cultures, who derived much of their prosperity from metalworking, have left us no written records, but we can get some idea of the impact of this earlier industrial revolution on Mediterranean life from the Greeks of the same period. The first surviving work of Greek literature, the *Iliad*, deals with the events leading up to the fall of Troy at the end of the Bronze Age, but at the funeral games in honor of Patroclus in two competitions, archery and the Homeric equivalent of putting the shot, the prizes are large lumps of pig iron. These may seem inappropriate as well as anachronistic for Bronze Age heroes, but Homer explains their usefulness: "Achilles placed down a massive lump of iron which mighty Eetion had once used as a throwing weight; the swift-footed god-like Achilles had killed him and loaded it aboard the ships with his other possessions. He stood up now and said to the Greeks: 'Up, those of you who want to try for this prize. The winner, however extensive his rich lands may be, will have its use for five whole years; neither his shepherd nor his plowman will need to go to the city for iron, but will have this to use.'" Achilles emphasizes the practical value of the prize, and with good reason. The old bronze tools and weapons, after all, were always liable to fracture and soon lost their cutting edge; furthermore, bronze required very high temperatures for casting. Iron could be forged at a lower temperature and gave better and longer-lasting results, and was in any case much more easily available. As we shall see, the arrival of the new technique gave a new impetus to the making of both farming and manufacturing tools and the improved agriculture and developing industries of the Villanovan communities of northern Italy between 900 and 700 BC are a direct result.

But before approaching the Villanovans and their neighbors, we must try to disentangle the end of the Bronze Age and the period of transition to the Iron Age, and unfortunately this is far from easy. Only future archaeological discoveries will settle many of the points at issue: for the present most of the period from 1200 to 900 BC remains confused, and scholarly disagreement is massive and often heated. The problem lies not only in understanding the period itself – which is hard enough – but in interpreting it in the light of the following centuries of Etruscan and Roman culture, where the evidence is much more complete, and about which therefore so much more is known. It is tempting to work backwards from this later period and use our knowledge of it to throw light on the earlier one, but this is liable to create fresh difficulties, of which the problem of the introduction into Italy of Indo-European is an example. With the glaring exception of the Etruscans, by Classical times all Italic people spoke languages that belonged to the linguistic family known as Indo-European, a family that includes most modern European languages and, in India, Sanskrit and related languages: the best-known example from ancient Italy is Latin. The Indo-European group of languages, however, seems to have originated in the steppes, and only spread to Europe during the period from 2000 to 1000 BC. When, then, during this period did an Indo-European language arrive in Italy, from where did it come, and who brought it? Some scholars believe that Indo-European dialects were brought by traders or settlers from the east, who crossed the Adriatic to Italy as early as 2000 BC. Others claim that the Villanovans themselves brought an Indo-European language with them when they arrived in north and central Italy over 1,000 years later; while still others believe that Villanovan culture did not arrive from elsewhere, but represents an evolved stage of an earlier Bronze Age culture which itself spoke an Indo-European dialect. All these are possible theories: the sad fact is, of course, that not a single written word has survived from the Villanovan period – let alone earlier – so that we have no certain evidence of any language in Italy before Classical times. On the basis of our present knowledge, therefore, the questions must remain unanswered.

On balance, it is probably simpler to take the archaeological evidence for

The major sites of Early Iron Age Italy.

the Late Bronze and Early Iron Ages as it stands, and not to try too hard to reconcile it with later developments: the case of the Etruscans provides a good illustration of how to lose sight of the real issues by working backwards from a later period, as we shall see.

Meanwhile, before turning to the end of the Bronze Age, a couple of warnings are in order. First, it is now clear that the development of culture by the introduction of new ideas, techniques and even languages is a much more complex process than our 19th-century predecessors thought, believing as they did that any important cultural change was produced by an invasion – usually warlike – from outside. Earlier scholars' theories of successive waves of invaders to explain cultural changes have been replaced in our day by a greater understanding of the ways in which societies develop. In particular, modern sociologists have been able to study the effects of outsiders of a high cultural and technological level upon a relatively primitive society. In Bronze Age or Early Iron Age Italy, for example, a small group of skilled metalworkers, perhaps even a single family, who moved to a simple agricultural society and settled there peacefully, would have produced a marked alteration in that society's ways, improving its agricultural methods by making better tools, changing its economic structure and as a result its social organization. If they also spoke a different language, that too might produce some changes in the speech of the established community. On the other hand, all these changes would not be in only one direction and undoubtedly the new settlers would adapt themselves to the established ways of the society. A new type of community would probably develop, and in a few generations it would be difficult to disentangle the separate elements that had gone into making it. In other words, cultures which may appear to make a break with the past do not always come into existence by arriving prepackaged from elsewhere and replacing their predecessors, but can be created either by a process of interaction between already existing ones or by the assimilation of an outside influence on the part of an established culture, creating a new amalgamation.

Finally it is important to remember that regional diversity has always been an Italian characteristic, as the most casual visitor to Italy can recognize. Even today, in spite of the Risorgimento, local loyalties are still stronger than national ties and are based upon genuine regional differences of culture, language and attitude. This diversity is certainly no new phenomenon: a Bolognese industrial worker and a Calabrian shepherd of today are probably no more different than were their Early Iron Age counterparts. The observation of Count Cavour, the architect of 19th-century Italian unity, that "having unified Italy it was necessary to unify the Italians," can be applied to just about any period of Italian history since the Bronze Age. Such variety makes for richness, of course, and local differences can be found in fields as diverse as architecture and food. On the other hand this spirit of separatism meant that different regions developed at different speeds, which inevitably slowed down the rate of intellectual and technological growth: the contrast between the organized, efficient north with contacts beyond the Alps and the conservative divided south is no new phenomenon in Italy. In this respect the Early Iron Age in Italy is very different from that of Greece, where in spite of local differences a single shared culture, based on shared language, technology and artistic styles, produced precisely the fruitful climate of ambition and competition that forms a thriving and creative society. Indeed, it was only the arrival of the

Greeks at the end of the 8th century BC that brought to Italy a number of basic cultural tools, including the alphabet, and no Italic people, including the Romans, ever recovered from the impact of Greek ideas. But already by then an Italic culture and style had developed, and to find their source we must return to the end of the Bronze Age.

The Late Bronze Age. By 1600 BC the disturbances of the Early Bronze Age had given way in southern Italy to a period of tranquillity and agricultural development. Excavation of sites of this period has produced very few weapons of either bronze or stone and the sites themselves were generally constructed without defenses, either natural or man-made. It seems that the inhabitants of the Apennine peninsula could settle down to an extended time of peace. Land was cultivated and the crops included wheat and barley; sheep, goats and cows were among the domestic animals in use. As well as farming, there had developed in the Early Bronze Age a strong tradition of animal rearing and this continued, with the result that some of the new settlements of this period are in mountainous regions, and were probably used as temporary summer camps: the herdsmen moved from their lowland villages in the spring, when the snow up in the mountains melted, to make use of the fresh grazing land, and returned home in the autumn.

The culture of this period is known as Apennine after the areas in which it first developed, but it spread gradually throughout much of Italy, arriving as far north as Bologna. The annual gatherings of shepherds and herdsmen who would meet in the summer at the grazing lands sharing their ideas and then returning to their respective villages obviously helped communication, and in spite of some local variations Apennine culture is remarkably consistent. In almost all Apennine communities the dead were buried rather than cremated. In general the materials used were limited. Bronze was known but used only rarely; as if to compensate, however, Apennine potters showed considerable imagination and a genuine aesthetic sense, using a wide variety of shapes and designs. They were clearly fascinated by the ways in which basic styles could be developed, and constantly found new and interesting ways of treating as mundane a feature as handles: these were sometimes treated abstractly and sometimes given the form of an animal's head – dog, cow or other.

This delight in visual effects and lack of conservatism is striking in its context. On the other hand, it is important to remember how isolated and undeveloped Apennine culture was in comparison with that of the eastern Mediterranean, whose sophisticated urban societies bore little resemblance to these simple agricultural communities. The years 1600 to 1400 BC mark the last and richest period of palace life at Knossos, and Minoan art of the time shows a range and imagination undreamed of in Bronze Age Italy. Even the Mycenaean traders from mainland Greece, who by 1400 BC had begun traveling widely in the west, made little impact: except for a trading post at Taranto, there is little evidence of Mycenaean contact with mainland Italy.

In contrast to this picture of Apennine stability, around 1500 BC there arrived in northern Italy, in the valley of the Po river between modern Parma and Bologna, a group of immigrants from north of the Alps, known as the Terramara people or, to give them their Italian name, the Terramaricoli. The discovery of the existence of these people was only made in the 19th century. Probably for centuries farmers in the Po valley

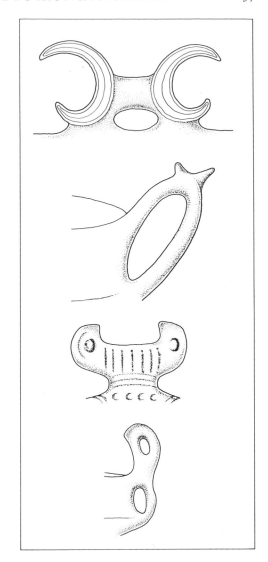

Types of bowl handle found in Bronze Age Italy. The top two handles are from Apennine pottery and show something of their range and variety. The elaborate curves are typical of southern Italy, while the large loop crowned with two small horns seems to reflect styles found further east around the Aegean. The other two examples come from northern sites: the horned type is found around Lake Garda, while the perforated style is characteristic of the eastern Veneto. After Barfield and Trump.

had used the rich dark earth from large mounds, known locally as *terremare* (black earth), to fertilize their fields; in the 19th century these mounds were systematically excavated and were found to contain the accumulated refuse of Bronze Age village settlements, piled up by their original inhabitants perhaps as a protection against flood. The effect of these discoveries on the study of prehistoric Italy in the late 19th and early 20th centuries was immense, if unfortunate, since the Terramaricoli were credited with an influence upon the period that followed them which we now know was vastly exaggerated. Much still remains controversial, but subsequent excavations have clarified the general picture.

The Terramaricoli came from central or eastern Europe, possibly Hungary, and unlike the Apennine people they showed exceptional skill in working bronze. Indeed, a considerable trade in bronze tools and ornaments developed between the Terramaricoli and Apennine people, and finds have been made the length of the east coast as far south as Taranto. Clearly there was interchange of both objects and ideas, since not only do we find an Apennine use of bone decorated with typical Terramara circle designs, but adoption by Terramara potters of Apennine motifs. In contrast to the Apennine people they cremated their dead: the ashes were placed in urns of poor quality and buried without the accompaniment of grave goods. In some cases the urns were packed closely together – one cemetery, at Casinalbo in Emilia, had dozens of urns stacked up in two levels – and this apparent indifference to the fate of the body after death has suggested to some a disbelief on their part in the afterlife.

It is in their use of cremation that the Terramara people most clearly foreshadowed the end of the Bronze Age, since one of the characteristics of the cultural transition to the Iron Age around 1000 BC was that almost the whole of Italy from the Alps to Sicily adopted the custom of cremation and urn burial; and many scholars during the 19th and early 20th centuries therefore claimed the later spread of cremation was a direct result of Terramara influence. This is not impossible, but it led to further claims that the Terramaricoli had arrived on the scene bringing not only the burial customs, but the culture and the language of the future Italy, and were in fact the first true Italic people. The leading Italian archaeologist of the late 19th century, Luigi Pigorini, claimed to see in the layout of the Terramara villages evidence of a strict grid plan similar to that of a Roman military camp, thereby demonstrating that the Terramaricoli were the founders of Rome and the ancestors of the Romans. As Massimo Pallottino, among the most distinguished archaeologists of our own day, was to complain half a century later, in this way the myth of Romulus and Remus was replaced in the name of "science" by the myth of the Terramaricoli. More recent opinion has tended to see Terramara culture as a relatively localized phenomenon which, although it developed trading connections with the south, remained limited to the Po valley.

Their way of life was certainly more sophisticated than that of the Apennine people. Their villages were far more carefully built and often covered several acres, and provision was made for defense against flooding by raising the ground level, thereby creating the large mounds which later farmers were to find so useful. The problem of flooding has always existed in the Po valley, and still does so today, but the advantage of being near the rivers, which were a major means of communication, must have compensated for the disadvantages. Nevertheless, many of the villages took the extra precaution of constructing earth ramparts buttressed by wooden beams; these beams, the traces of which were preserved by the dampness of the ground, were found by the first excavators, and misled their finders into reconstructing whole villages built on pile-supported platforms and standing above the plain around, rather in the manner of the contemporary transalpine lake villages. The agricultural level of these communities was high: the range of crops was considerable, including wheat and beans, and the fruit eaten included pears, apples, cherries and pistachio nuts. Furthermore, among the domesticated animals in use was the horse, which had yet to be introduced into southern Italy. As we saw earlier, the Terramaricoli traded widely in bronze, increasing their contacts with the south, and these peaceful exchanges continued throughout the Late Bronze Age as new metal supplies from southern Tuscany became available.

It is still difficult to provide a final assessment of the contribution of the Terramara culture to the development of early Italy. Their efficiency, ability in metalworking (and thereby in making weapons) and use of cremation are certainly reminiscent of their successors, the Villanovans. On the other hand, the fragmentation of Early Iron Age culture makes a single unifying Terramara influence improbable.

Transition to the Iron Age. At the very end of the Bronze Age, around 1100 BC, the pattern of life throughout Italy changed. Cremation, which had hitherto been confined to the Terramara people, spread throughout Italy, and urn-field cemeteries are found as far south as Apulia and Sicily. The urns themselves are often biconical in shape and the bronze pins and razors buried with them are of a kind not found earlier in Italy. In general both bronze and pottery show characteristics familiar from central and eastern Europe, and in some cases the objects were actually imported. A superb bronze cup found near Civitavecchia with a hoard of other bronze objects, which is now in the Museo Pigorini, Rome, was almost certainly brought from central Europe; it is decorated with a beaten design and the handle is crowned with a stylized bull's head. There has been much debate as to how these new ideas arrived in Italy. Some believe that they were brought by a new influx of immigrants either from the north across the Alps or the east across the Adriatic. Others see these apparently new ideas as in fact a late development of the old Apennine culture, while others, as we saw, relate them to the arrival 500 years earlier of the Terramara people. We must be cautious of reverting to the idea of invading hordes, but certainly the century before the arrival of iron around 1000 BC shows evidence of strong links to the north of the Alps. This new transitional culture, which seems to foreshadow the Iron Age rather than belong to the Bronze Age, is called proto-Villanovan, but the name is a little misleading: it must be remembered that it precedes not only the Villanovans, but all the other disparate cultures of Iron Age Italy.

The new uniformity was, however, not to last long. Society in Italy was changing: agriculture never lost its importance (and indeed has kept it to the present), but with the development of metalworking and industries, it was no longer the only means of existence. As small villages began to band together into larger communities a form of civic life began to develop, and with it local differences became emphasized and strengthened. As the Iron Age dawned, in the south, in Apulia, there seems to have been a regression to earlier conservative ways, with a striking return to inhumation instead of cremation, and old Apennine-style pottery. Elsewhere in Italy new

Bronze biconical urn with helmet lid, Badisches Landesmuseum, Karlsruhe. The use of human figures, here perhaps musicians participating in the funeral ceremony, is reminiscent of that on the bronze amphora from Bisenzio on p. 66.

cultures began to appear: on the east coast the Picenes began to develop their own highly characteristic society, while in the northwest the Ligurians and in the northeast the Veneti are examples of other widely diverging cultures. We shall look briefly at these two later, but first we must turn to the culture which dominated most of north and central Italy, the Villanovans.

The Villanovans. Villanovan culture takes its name from the Iron Age cemetery which was discovered and excavated in 1853 near the modern village of Villanova, some 4 miles to the east of Bologna. Finds from this and other cemeteries nearby first established the general characteristics of a culture which appeared, with variations, in a number of parts of Italy during the years from 900 to 500 BC; and "Villanovan" serves as a convenient label for these, as long as we remember that the Villanovans of Bologna may have shared a common culture with their counterparts in Tuscany or Campania but not necessarily a common racial origin or development.

The area around Bologna provides us with the most vivid picture of the growing urbanization and sophistication of life in the Early Iron Age, mainly because up to now it has produced most of our information. Bologna itself seems to have been the most prosperous center in northern Italy, growing rapidly in size and population between 900 and 750 BC, and remained Villanovan in character until as late as 500 BC, when the Etruscans, who had already replaced the Villanovans further south in Tuscany, moved north to the Po valley and established a political confederation there. Bologna, under its Etruscan name of Felsina, formed a part of this, and archaeological evidence shows a strong Etruscan influence.

Although much remains to be discovered about the city itself in Villanovan times, excavation of the huge cemeteries around its edges has uncovered many thousands of tombs, and the material from these has been used by archaeologists to reconstruct the economic and social organization of the community. The change from the relatively simple burials of 900–800 BC to the much richer graves of the following century, with their elaborate ash urns, bronze and iron jewelry and decorated vessels, shows how fast wealth was spreading – and how broadly throughout the society. Clearly, prosperity was not just limited to a ruling class but was becoming much more diffused, and a class of successful tradesmen and manufacturers was developing. The cause of this economic boom is not hard to find, for the Villanovans put their outstanding craftsmanship in both bronze and iron to good use, and production and distribution were on a massive scale. The enlarging market required increasing quantities of raw material, and as their trade with their neighbors to the south developed, supplies of copper and iron were imported from Tuscany. The picture of a flourishing economy based on the twin supports of manufacturing and trade, coupled with urban development and a rising middle class, seems almost reminiscent of the great northern industrial centers of 19th-century England, and one writer has called Iron Age Bologna "the Birmingham of early Italy."

The scale of productivity is most vividly illustrated by a single chance find: in 1877, near the church of San Francesco in the center of Bologna itself, was found a single huge clay storage jar containing the staggering number of 14,841 bronze objects, presumably collected to be melted down and reused. This hoard now fills an entire room in Bologna's Museo

Civico, and the range of objects is revealing. Many are farming or manufacturing tools, including 412 sickles and 398 chisels, and there are no fewer than 3,206 *fibulae* (or brooch pins), but there are very few weapons – only 19 swords, for example. Work and personal adornment seem to have been more important – and more popular – than war. Indeed such an immense industrial expansion would only have been possible in an atmosphere of relative peace, which was fortunate since Bologna itself lies in a position that is convenient for trade rather than for defense: it is on level ground, in an exposed position, with only the south protected by hills.

Hoards like the one from San Francesco are occasionally found elsewhere in central Italy, and provide archaeologists with important examples of material not found in tombs; for the rest our information is drawn almost entirely from the excavation of cemeteries. Very little is known about Villanovan architecture and town planning. Only in the last few years have Villanovan habitations been discovered, and then often by chance: when a pedestrian underpass was being dug in the very center of Bologna, leading from Piazza Nettuno to Via Rizzoli, the workmen came upon traces of Villanovan huts, together with remains from Roman Bologna. In this case it was possible to preserve the finds *in situ* and leave them as a reminder to traffic-dodging Bolognesi of their past, but the problem of the recovery and preservation of earlier stages in the life of cities such as Bologna is growing as the cities themselves grow, and new pressures develop. Sometimes it is possible to excavate even in urban areas – in 1973 an early 6th-century BC Etruscan sanctuary was uncovered near the University of Bologna Faculty of Engineering – but in general city land is too valuable to turn over to the archaeologists and economic considerations come first. The Villanovans would have probably agreed.

For the moment, therefore, our knowledge of Early Iron Age Bologna is mainly limited to the Villanovan way of death. The great cemeteries to the east and west of the city were in use from the 9th to the 6th centuries BC, and their thousands of graves have provided a wealth of material, most of it now in the Museo Civico. From 900 to 750 BC the dead were generally cremated: the charred fragments of bone were collected from the pyre and

Above: Bronze belt from a tomb in the Benacci cemetery near Bologna, 8th century BC. Length 42 cm. The elaborate and fanciful decoration, with ducks and stylized duck heads, is clearly influenced by the Hallstatt culture north of the Alps. One of the finest surviving examples of Villanovan metalwork, the belt is now in the Museo Civico, Bologna.

Below: Diagram of *pozzo* burial. The biconical urn containing the ashes of the deceased is placed in a small pit or *pozzetto* dug in the bottom of the larger *pozzo*. The *pozzetto* is then closed with a stone slab and the large hole filled in. After Ghirardini.

placed in an urn which was then lowered into a well, or *pozzo*, at the bottom of which had been dug a smaller hole or *pozzetto*. The urn was placed in this lower hole and the top sealed with a stone slab. The urns themselves are among the most characteristic of Villanovan objects. Most of them are made of dark clay and resemble large storage jars of the kind called "two-storied" – a high, slightly bulging neck sits on a broad body that bulges below where the neck joins. In almost all cases they have only one handle, although they must have been heavy and difficult to lower into position without a second one. This was obviously deliberate, however, since when an urn had originally been made with two handles, one of them was broken off before the urn was buried. Presumably it was important to its users that an urn to be used for burial could no longer serve a practical use for the living, that in a sense it too was dead.

Villanovan burial urns. These urns have a number of different types of lid. The simplest consists of a bowl with incurving lip and a single handle, which was turned upside down and placed over the mouth of the urn. This is the most common form, but others are more elaborate and, thereby, more informative archaeologically. In some cases instead of a bowl a bronze helmet was placed over the urn, although the Villanovans sometimes economized by using the model of a helmet made of clay; this retained the idea but saved burying the original. The bronze helmets themselves are finely made and often very beautiful: they are either crested or round, like skull caps, and decorated with elaborate designs generally made up of circles and disks, and at the top there is often an attachment for a plume. These helmet-urns, with their stylized bodies decorated with geometric designs and the helmets creating the suggestion of a human head, seem almost to represent the presence of their owners, and it is difficult to believe that the Villanovans themselves did not to some degree see them as anthropomorphic. As other examples will show, the ability to endow inanimate objects with a life and personality of their own is found elsewhere in early Italic art, and also among the Etruscans. To our eyes, accustomed to Greek art and its almost obsessive concern with the human form at its purest and most perfect, these urns may seem strange, particularly in view of the fact that during the period of their use Greek ideas were becoming widespread in Italy. But in spite of the impact of the Greeks, Italic art was to retain its love of the fantastic and even the grotesque. In a sense the concepts behind much of Villanovan, Etruscan or Samnite art are basically non-intellectual: there is little of the Greek interest in form and proportion, and instead an emphasis on an instinctive expression that at times can seem almost violent. But if Italic art is in one sense primitive, it is certainly not simple-minded. Even these Villanovan urns sometimes show a surprising number of levels of meaning: a bronze lid from a Villanovan tomb at Tarquinia, for example, not only represents the helmet itself, but at the same time evokes the image of its wearer by its decoration of circles and disks which were clearly intended to suggest a human face. The artist has remained true to his world, however, and the depiction is completely stylized, with no trace of individuality, and is filled out with other decorative motifs, including birds' heads which are themselves stylized. A class is represented, not an individual person, that of professional warriors or warrior-farmers. Even if on the whole Villanovan life was peaceful enough, vigilance must have been necessary, and warriors would have been honored members of society.

The bodies of the urns, with their abstract designs, gave their makers further opportunities to indulge their fantasies. The designs were produced in a variety of ways: lines were frequently incised with a comb-like tool to produce a series of geometric designs using parallel lines, while in other cases rope or small stamps were used to make impression on the clay while it was still wet, metal studs and strips were sometimes stuck into the surface, and on a few occasions thick white paint was applied. By combining several of these techniques an artist could achieve a rich and complex texture: an urn from Tarquinia, now in the Museo Pigorini, Rome, looks like a kind of Villanovan collage.

Another kind of Villanovan urn is found most commonly in the area of Latium around the future Rome, although examples have also been excavated at sites further north. These are called hut-urns, and take the form of oval or rectangular houses, generally provided with a door which can be fastened with a crossbar – presumably to protect the ashes inside. Side windows are sometimes painted on, and the roofs are gabled with eaves projecting all round; the holes under the gable ends probably represent air vents. Without other archaeological evidence it would have been impossible to know if these hut-urns really resembled actual house types or were merely imaginary, stylized ones, but by good fortune the foundations of a group of Early Iron Age huts have been excavated in Rome itself, on the Palatine hill, and these corroborate to a remarkable degree the form of the hut-urns. Although most of the urns themselves are of clay, some bronze examples have been found, including a superb and

Above: Villanovan biconical urn, c. 800 BC. Vatican Museums. Height 43 cm. The narrow parallel lines forming the meander design were probably incised with a comb. Note that there is only one handle.

Above left: Villanovan hut-urn from Vulci, c. 800 BC. Villa Giulia, Rome. Height 34 cm. The eaves of the gabled roof overhang and there are smoke holes at each end. The incised rectangle on the side wall is perhaps intended to suggest a window. The top ridge, where the roof beams meet, is decorated with a row of horns which may be derived from the stylized bird motif.

Opposite: Bronze Villanovan crested helmet (*top*) from Tarquinia, 9th century. Height 36 cm. The three holes at the base of the rim are for attaching cheek pieces or a chin strap. Museo Archeologico, Florence. Cap helmet (*bottom*) designed in the form of a stylized human face, late 8th century, from a Villanovan tomb at Tarquinia. Height 16 cm. The face may have represented a Villanovan war god who could be relied on to protect its wearer in battle.

elaborately ornamented one from Vulci, now in the Villa Giulia, Rome:
the central beam is decorated with what are probably stylized birds' heads,
a motif which occurs frequently in Villanovan art, and is used by some
archaeologists as proof that the Villanovans came originally from north of
the Alps, where the birds' head motif seems to have originated. This hut-
urn from Vulci may in turn help to explain a strange bronze object now in
the Yale University Art Gallery: it consists of a curved bronze band, over
3½ feet long, to which is attached a row of 13 bronze birds, seven facing one
way and six the other. The whole piece may have been used to decorate the
central beam of an actual hut, rather as in the Vulci model, although it
seems rather delicate to have been placed outside; perhaps it was hung
inside.

Another bronze hut-urn now in the Metropolitan Museum in New
York has a different decoration on its roof: it is crowned with what seems to
be the outline of a boat with a high stern, while above the door is placed the
head of a horned animal, curiously like the stuffed heads so dear to hunters.
We can, of course, only guess at the significance of these, but it is interesting
to note that the boat is often found in eastern art as a symbol of the journey
to the next life, and this motif is also used by the Etruscans.

The helmet- and hut-urns, then, tell us something about their makers
and owners; two other urns, both from the end of the Villanovan period,
illustrate something of the Villanovan vision of the world. The first, from
Montescudaio in northwest Tuscany, where it was buried around 650 BC, is
made of clay and decorated on the sides with the same kind of patterns we
have seen on earlier urns, although here they are in low relief – a sign of
growing Etruscan influence. What gives the urn its unique character,
though, are the free-standing figures on its lid and above the handle, a rare
example in early Italic art of a scene showing human activity. We meet one
of the characters twice, once over the handle, where he sits quietly and a
little glumly, dressed in a short-sleeved tunic, his hands resting on his knees,
and again on the lid, where he is sitting at a three-legged table which is
laden with food; there are two large vases on the ground (one is now
missing), and to his left a servant girl stands on a low stool. The scene is
clearly that of the funeral banquet which formed, as we know from the
Etruscan tomb paintings, an important part of the funeral ceremony, and
the principal character on the urn must be the dead man himself, joining in
the banquet in effigy on the lid while his ashes lie in the jar beneath. What is
striking about the scene is its complete lack of self-consciousness: its maker

Top: Bird ornament, bronze. Yale University
Art Gallery. Length 125 cm. One bird is
missing: originally seven faced in each direction.
The function of the object is uncertain. It might
have been used as a house ornament, to hang
from the central beam inside; alternatively it
perhaps formed part of a bronze cart of the type
used for the ritual burning of incense.

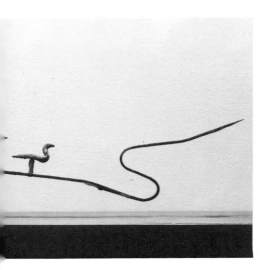

Above: Bronze Villanovan hut-urn, c.800 BC. Metropolitan Museum, New York. The roof is decorated with a high-sterned boat, and over the door there is an animal head.

Right: Clay urn from Montescudaio, early 7th century BC. Museo Archeologico, Florence. Height c. 49 cm.

Bronze vessel from the cemetery of Olmo Bello, Bisenzio, late 8th or early 7th century BC. Villa Giulia, Rome. Height 32 cm. It is a fine example of late Villanovan bronze work, for which Bisenzio seems to have been a center.

lived at a time increasingly dominated by the new artistic ideas introduced into Italy by the Greeks, but he shows no sign of interest in them. The figures are depicted with a directness and a simplicity that seem almost childlike, and the Italian scholar Bianchi Bandinelli has drawn an interesting parallel with the primitive art of Precolumbian America and the Ashanti culture of Africa.

The second piece is from the late 8th century BC and was found in a tomb near Bisenzio, to the north of Tarquinia, where five cemeteries have been excavated, ranging in date from the end of the 8th to the beginning of the 6th century BC. Large numbers of bronze objects were found, including this amphora, which in comparison with the urn from Montescudaio shows a greater sophistication of form and a higher level of craftsmanship; but the scene on the lid is if anything even more "primitive" and powerful. In the center is chained a sinister and mysterious animal, possibly a bear but more probably a mythological creature, and around it there move two circles of men, most of them armed, in a kind of measured dance. This procession of warriors around the central figure, which represents a divinity or perhaps even Death itself, is only interrupted by the appearance in the lower of the two circles of a farmer who is driving a long-horned ox; the animal is yoked and the farmer is on his way to work. The appearance of this symbol of peace in the middle of the violence of the war dance is extraordinarily disturbing; indeed, the scene as a whole, whatever its religious significance may be, makes an impression out of all proportion to the technical resources employed. Although the small figures are simply, even crudely, modeled, there is a tension in the scene which suggests a darker side to late Villanovan life. This vividness of impact and lack of subtlety of execution are typical of much Italic art.

Villanovan art retained these characteristics even when most exposed to Greek ideas, as is shown by a number of finds from the recently discovered Villanovan cemetery at Pontecagnano, near Salerno, which is still being excavated. Although many Greek and eastern objects have been found, and Greek influence was clearly strong, a number of important pieces are clearly of local manufacture and inspiration. Among them there is the conical lid to an urn, on top of which are two figures, male and female, with hands and feet that seem more like paws or claws, and huge, immensely prolonged noses; their eyes are represented by the same kind of disk design which we saw used on the helmet from Tarquinia. The creatures seem half-human, half-animal; they perhaps represent guardians watching over and protecting the urn, and although clearly part of their strange quality is due to the extreme roughness with which they have been modeled, they too, like the other examples, have a remarkable and grotesque power. This is emphasized by the combination of abstract design (the circles for eyes) and realism (the noses, which if monstrous are certainly recognizable) – a combination which, as we have seen, is characteristically Italic.

So far we have been dealing with the burial urns, which because of their immense religious significance are objects least likely to be influenced by foreign ideas, but elsewhere the Villanovans showed a greater interest in Greek ideas. In the 8th and 7th centuries BC small wiry geometric bronze figurines were made, reminiscent of Greek "geometric" bronzes, and clearly influenced by Greek models. Even here, however, the Villanovans produced their own versions with a typical disregard for the basic requirements of naturalism: the figure of a girl on top of a candelabrum found at Vetulonia has her arms elongated and distorted in order to make two large abstract triangles, one on each side of her. Pieces like this might seem the result merely of faulty and undeveloped technique, were it not that the aesthetic principles we see in them recur at later periods in the art of the Samnites, the Etruscans and other Italic peoples, who often retain, even in their most superbly crafted pieces, the sense of the abstract and the grotesque that emerges in this early period.

Nor is this fantasy reserved for the treatment of humans. The commonest motif of all in Villanovan art is that of the bird which, as we saw earlier, is probably derived from the bird designs of central Europe and the Balkans. Sometimes the Villanovan birds were used decoratively, as in the bronze hut-urn from Vulci, but often they were combined with other animal forms to produce typically Villanovan hybrid creations. A vase from one of the Bologna cemeteries shows a horse and rider placed on a creature that has the body of a bird but the head of an ox; the decoration consists once again of incised disk designs, but these are carefully arranged to suggest the wings of the bird. In another example, this time from Tarquinia, the body of a bird has been turned into a small carriage, set on wheels, and given the head of a deer (or possibly an ox). The body itself is hollowed out, and closed by a perforated lid that also has the form of a bird's body and has been given its own animal head. The object was probably used as an incense burner, and again combines the qualities, familiar by now, of abstractness, fantasy and realism.

All these pieces were found in the tombs, buried with the urns, and even if they represent only one aspect of Villanovan life they are immensely valuable in the information they provide. In the case of a society which has left no written legacy, archaeologists must derive their conclusions from evidence such as this; and the Villanovan graves provide us with considerable insight into their lives. Indeed they do more, because they demonstrate that, although by the end of the 6th century BC Villanovan culture had ceased to exist throughout Italy, it was to prove a powerful influence upon their successors, the Etruscans.

The Este culture and the Ligurians. By 750 BC, when the Villanovans of Bologna were at the height of their prosperity, another culture had established itself to the northeast of the Po, in the area now called the Veneto. Since the major settlement of these people was at Ateste, the modern name of which is Este, they are generally called the Atestine or Este people, although they are sometimes known as the *situla* people, after the objects for which they are most famous, decorated bronze buckets called *situlae*. Living so far north they were, unlike the Villanovans, relatively unaffected by the rise and fall of the Etruscans, in spite of considerable cultural exchange, and even the growing power of Rome was felt politically rather than culturally; their language, Venetic, is closely related to Latin and this must have helped the development of friendly relations with the Romans. But even though a long period of alliance was followed in 182 BC by their willing acceptance of Roman political control, for most of their history they remained culturally independent: their closest ties were, in fact, with the north and east rather than the Italian peninsula, and situla art has been found as far north as Austria and across the Adriatic to the east in Slovenia.

The bronze situlae themselves were probably used to hold wine and they and other bronze objects – dagger sheaths, belt buckles, cups – were decorated with scenes which give a vivid picture of their makers' daily lives. Like the Villanovans and the Etruscans, the Este people were strongly influenced by motifs coming from the east: a belt buckle in the Museo Archeologico, Este, shows a winged monster with a human leg dangling from its mouth, an Oriental motif which also appears in Etruscan art. But these outside influences were assimilated to create a truly local style, and on pieces like the Benvenuti situla, made around 600 BC and also in the Museo Archeologico, Este, Orientalizing sphinxes and griffins are combined

Vessel in the shape of a bird with the head of an ox from the Cava della Pozzolana necropolis, Cerveteri, 8th–7th century BC. Villa Giulia, Rome. Note the similarity of decoration to the piece opposite.

with scenes of battle and of daily life which provide the archaeologist with remarkably detailed information on a wide variety of aspects of Este culture. From this and other examples we can see how these people went to war, what games they played and how they made love; there are scenes of banqueting, of hunting and of farming.

A remarkable piece now in Bologna is chiefly valuable for its illustration of the high level of technology of the Este people, but at the same time it provides an interesting example of how the process of excavation needs always to be followed up by examination and restoration under laboratory conditions. In 1874 the tomb of a woman between 30 and 40 years old was discovered in one of Bologna's Villanovan cemeteries, containing a number of gold objects (for which the tomb was named the "Tomba degli Ori") and a small rattle or *tintinnabulum* made of two sheets of bronze fastened together, a find with no visible decoration and apparently little significance. This rattle has recently been cleaned in the laboratory of the Museo Civico, Bologna, and scenes in low relief, hitherto invisible, have been discovered on both sides: we now know that it was made by the situla people around 600 BC, and probably sold to the wealthy Villanovan matron

Askos (or flask) from the Benacci cemetery, Bologna, 7th century BC. Museo Civico, Bologna. Height c. 18 cm. It is one of a series of bird vessels found in northern and central Italy which were probably influenced by similar motifs to the north of the Alps in the urnfields of central Europe.

Clay bird vessel on wheels from the Pelà cemetery at Este, 7th century BC. Museo Archeologico, Este. Like the examples from Tarquinia and Bologna it illustrates the influence of northern motifs.

whose tomb this was. The two sides illustrate the entire process of wool working from cleaning and carding to spinning and weaving, including the most elaborate picture of a loom to have survived from the ancient world; it is two stories high and is being worked by a woman seated comfortably in a high-backed armchair.

This and other scenes, peopled by the characteristic round-cheeked, long-nosed figures, show a liveliness and often a narrative quality which is extremely rare in early Italic art, and which remains distinctive as late as the 4th century BC. A shrine of this period has been excavated at Este, dedicated to the goddess Reithia, a local goddess of healing, in which were found a number of small bronze votive figurines. Although these show clear evidence of growing contacts with the Etruscans and other Italic peoples, they still retain the vividness of detail which is characteristic of situla art.

In contrast to the Este people, the Ligurians present a much barer picture, and very little has survived of these people who lived in the northwest corner of Italy, comprising modern Liguria and parts of southwest

Piedmont. So little indeed is known of this region that some scholars do not even believe that it is possible to speak of a separate and distinct Ligurian culture. The Romans, whose contacts with them were based on 200 years of bitter fighting, thought of them as barely civilized, living in caves and primitive huts, although their beer and honey had some reputation in antiquity. Archaeological evidence is very scanty and, until recently, non-existent for the Early Iron Age. In 1959, however, an 8th-century BC cemetery was discovered in one of the few fertile valleys of Liguria, at Chiavari, and the material from it combines Etruscan and Atestine characteristics with features of its own. Cremation was practiced and the clay ash urns were decorated with a wide variety of designs showing abstract patterns, humans and animals, and sometimes had animal figures in relief.

From the same period come a number of statue menhirs, or stone slabs carved to resemble standing human figures. The use of such slabs, possibly as grave markers or representations of deities, is extremely old, and similar examples from southern France and Corsica date to the end of the Neolithic period. The weapons carried by the figures in these Ligurian examples make it certain that they date to the Iron Age, over 2,000 years later, but why the Ligurians should have revived so ancient and obsolete a form is impossible to say. Nor is their purpose clear, since they are not found in cemeteries or near graves. Their schematic style and air of isolation serve as a reminder that the Ligurians are probably the most "mysterious" of all Italic peoples, certainly far more so than the "mysterious" Etruscans.

Statue menhirs. The roughly carved one (*left*) comes from near Merano in the central Alpine region and probably dates to the late third millennium BC. Other examples of the same type and period have been found in France and in southern Italy to the south of the Tavoliere plain. The more recognizably human menhir (*right*) is from Liguria, and is one of a series which were almost certainly produced in the Early Iron Age. Their purpose is unknown, since they were not found associated with burials, and their relationship to the examples of 2,000 years earlier is uncertain. Museo Civico, Merano, and Museo Lunense, La Spezia.

Situla Art

The importance of the Situla peoples as a link between cultures north of the Alps and the Etruscans and others of central and southern Italy is becoming increasingly clear. Recent studies of Orientalizing motifs and Etruscan costume styles which appear in situla art indicate that its inspiration is by no means exclusively transalpine or transadriatic. Nevertheless the Atestine culture of the 6th and 5th centuries BC is most closely linked with the Illyrians to the east and north: they represent a similar society, ruled by chieftains at whose feasts the situlae were used, and both produced an artistic style that combined traditionalism with vividness of narrative depiction.

1

1 The Bologna situla, formerly believed to be from the Certosa cemetery. Museum of Art, Rhode Island School of Design, Providence. Height 26·6 cm. This example shows scenes of music and banqueting, and is especially interesting for the range of costumes worn, which seem to distinguish between social classes. The wide-brimmed hats indicate the chieftains, while other participants in the feasts and sports wear what looks like a knitted beret.

2 The Certosa situla, found in the Certosa cemetery near Bologna, c. 500 BC. Museo Civico, Bologna. Height 32 cm. Either manufactured locally or, more probably, imported from the north, it is one of the very finest examples of situla art. The top and bottom registers are decorative, showing a procession of soldiers and, below, a series of fantastic animals. Between them are two registers which give an amazingly vivid picture of aspects of daily life. We see a funeral procession, complete with sacrificial victim, on the upper of the two and two separate episodes on the lower: a musical competition between two chieftains and a party returning from the hunt.

3 and 4 The Benvenuti situla and grave goods found with it. Museo Archeologico, Este. Height of situla 32 cm. The bronze necklaces and fibulae decorated with animals can be dated to around 575 BC, and the situla is probably contemporary with them.

5 Bronze situla lid from Rebato, near Lake Como. Decorated with animal figures, it was probably imported from the Veneto into northwest Italy. It was discovered in the grave of a warrior who belonged to the culture known as Golasecca. After Ducati.

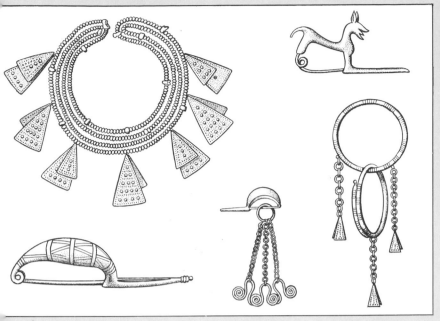

3

5

6

4

7

6 Beaker in the shape of a boot from the Nazari cemetery, Este, 6th century BC. Museo Archeologico, Este.

7 Pottery urn of situla shape from the Benvenuti cemetery at Este, early 6th century BC. Museo Archeologico, Este. It is decorated with applied bronze studs, presumably to provide a cheap imitation of the more expensive bronze situlae. Decorations of this kind, which are sometimes also found on Villanovan biconical urns, were probably inspired by similar techniques used on pottery north of the Alps in central Europe.

8 and 14 Two small decorated plaques: the larger of the two is 10·5 cm high, and shows a warrior with round shield, plumed helmet and two lances. The other one, showing the figure of a woman, is engraved rather than embossed. Museo Archeologico, Este.

9 Belt buckle from Este, 6th century BC. Museo Archeologico, Este. The motif of the human leg dangling from an animal's mouth is also found in Etruscan art. Its presence here is perhaps further evidence of contact between the Este people and the Etruscans, although both peoples may have borrowed the motif from a common Orientalizing source.

10, 11 and 12 Votive statuettes from the sanctuary of Reithia, 4th–3rd century BC. Museo Archeologico, Este. They were left as offerings to the goddess, who seems to have possessed powers of healing, and stylistically show the influence of contemporary Etruscan bronzes, presumably introduced by way of the nearby Etruscan city of Adria. Note the local costume worn by the woman.

13 Bronze *tintinnabulum* from the Tomb of the Gold Objects, Bologna, c. 600 BC. Museo Civico, Bologna. Height 11·5 cm. Although found in a Villanovan context, this piece is probably from Este, and shows in great detail the process of wool-working. After Ducati.

8

9

10

13

11

12

14

4 CENTRAL ITALY · THE ETRUSCANS AND THEIR NEIGHBORS

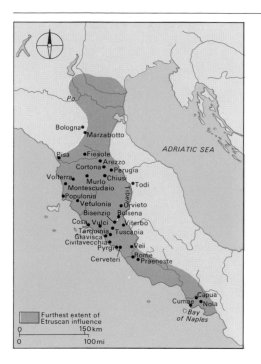

Above: Etruscan settlements in central Italy.

Opposite: Terracotta statue of Apollo from the sanctuary of Portonaccio at Veii, now in the Villa Giulia, Rome. Late 6th or early 5th century BC. Height 180 cm. Discovered in 1916 together with other terracotta statues and fragments, the Apollo of Veii played a large part in stimulating interest in Etruscan art. Its facial features show a characteristically Etruscan version of the Greek archaic smile.

More is known about the Etruscans than any other people of pre-Roman Italy – ironically enough for a culture whose popular reputation is founded on its mystery. The beginnings of a scholarly interest in Etruscology can be traced back to the 18th century, and recent years have seen a number of major new discoveries. Yet for many of their modern admirers the appeal of the Etruscans seems as much based on the apparent mystery surrounding their origins and language as on the immediacy of their art or the sophistication of their culture, a mystery which contrasts agreeably with the much clearer picture we have of the Greek and Roman worlds. Even a writer as self-consciously "intellectual" as Aldous Huxley emphasizes this romantic, mysterious aspect when in his story "After the Fireworks" he takes his hero and heroine to the Villa Giulia in Rome:

"A tall statue towered over her. 'The Apollo of Veii,' he explained. 'And really, you know, it is the most beautiful statue in the world. Each time I see it, I'm more firmly convinced of that.'

"Dutifully, Pamela stared. The God stood there on his pedestal, one foot advanced, erect in his draperies. He had lost his arms, but the head was intact and the strange Etruscan face was smiling, enigmatically smiling."

The awe of the unknown becomes, in D. H. Lawrence's *Etruscan Places*, a barely controlled irritation with the archaeologists who seek to explain the inexplicable and reveal the mysteries:

"Who wants object-lessons about vanished races? What one wants is a contact. The Etruscans are not a theory or a thesis. If they are anything, they are an *experience* . . . And the experience is always spoilt. Museums, museums, museums, object-lessons rigged out to illustrate the unsound theories of archaeologists, crazy attempts to coordinate and get into a fixed order that which has no fixed order and will not be coordinated! It is sickening . . . what one wants is the actual vital touch. I don't want to be 'instructed', nor do many other people."

Etruscan Places is a magnificent evocation of the places themselves and of Lawrence's reactions to them, but it certainly cannot be accused of providing instruction. Nonetheless, Lawrence's warning is salutary and the student of Etruscology who does try to coordinate, or at least to understand, can only hope that a fuller grasp of the breadth of Etruscan culture, and a more complete knowledge of the Etruscans' relationship to their contemporaries, will help to provide the "vital touch" which Lawrence demanded.

Origins of the Etruscans. There can be little doubt that the Etruscans' attractive air of mystery is due in large measure to the question of their origins, and although we are chiefly concerned here with the actual part they played in the development of pre-Roman Italy, a brief look at this

problem is necessary. Who were the Etruscans and where did they come from? Few issues in the ancient world have been more heatedly debated, from the Roman period to the present. In a sense the problem is not an archaeological one. A study of Etruscan culture limited strictly to their material remains shows a cultural pattern that seems to develop naturally out of the previous Villanovan period. The major areas of Etruscan expansion, including Veii, Tarquinia, Cerveteri and Vulci, were earlier centers of Villanovan culture, and many of the characteristic aspects of the early stages of Etruscan culture as it appears around 700 BC are found also in the last years of the Villanovans: the introduction of inhumation as well as or instead of cremation; the use of chamber tombs, either constructed or cut out of rock to hold the burials, instead of the earlier pits (*pozzi*) or trenches; the importation of foreign objects such as Egyptian scarab seals showing increasing contacts with the outside world – all these are as characteristic of the end of the Villanovan period in central Italy as of the early Etruscan. It is true that, in contrast with Villanovan art, from 700 BC Etruscan art shows very pronounced eastern characteristics, but this Orientalizing element is found throughout the Mediterranean at the same time, most notably in Greece itself. Certainly the arrival of the Greeks in Italy in the middle of the 8th century BC must have done much to spread Orientalizing ideas and styles in the west. The script used by the Etruscans, for example, was based on the Greek alphabet in use by the late 8th century BC at the newly founded colony of Cumae, on the bay of Naples, an alphabet which the Greeks themselves shortly before had adopted from a Phoenician script and had brought to Italy. Furthermore, the Etruscans were certainly not the only people in Italy whose art was Orientalizing in style: we have already seen something of the Este culture's use of eastern motifs, and in the south the people of both Campania and Sicily were clearly influenced by Orientalizing styles introduced by the Greeks.

For all these reasons some scholars have argued that Etruscan culture was not brought to Italy by the arrival of new immigrants from abroad, but was a natural outgrowth and development of Villanovan culture, and claim that the Etruscans were, in fact, autochthonous (or indigenous) to Italy. Unfortunately, although this theory of autochthonous origins is supported by a large body of archaeological evidence, it does not take into account a number of other facts which present crucial difficulties. The first of these, and by no means the least significant, is that just about every Greek or Roman writer who discussed the Etruscans believed that they arrived in Italy from the east, in most accounts from Lydia in Asia Minor, bringing their culture with them. The most detailed account of an Etruscan migration is provided by the Greek historian of the 5th century BC, Herodotus, who describes their arrival in Italy and explains how they acquired the name by which they were known to the Greeks:

"According to the story, in the reign of Atys, son of Manes, a terrible famine occurred throughout Lydia; the Lydians carried on as long as they could, but when things got no better they began to look for something to help and came up with a number of devices. It was during this time that they invented dice, knucklebones, ball games and other games (but not checkers). They used these to distract them from their hunger by, on alternate days, playing continuously one whole day so that they would not think about food, and eating on the following day without playing. In this way they got through 18 years. Things got worse, however, rather than better, and the king therefore divided all the Lydians into two groups and drew lots to decide which should stay and which should emigrate, putting himself at the head of those who were to remain and appointing his son, who was called Tyrrhenus, as the leader of those who had to leave. Those Lydians whose lot it was to leave went down to Smyrna and built boats on to which they loaded all their possessions and sailed away to seek a life elsewhere. After sailing past many lands they came to Umbria in Italy where they built cities and still live to this day, changing their name from Lydians to Tyrrhenians after the king's son Tyrrhenus who had led them."

It is easy to dismiss this story as a typical fable of the kind often found in the early historians, with a wealth of lively but uncircumstantial detail; and in any case there is something wrong with Herodotus' chronology, which places the migration in the middle of the 13th century BC. Nonetheless, the fact remains that the common opinion of the Etruscans' neighbors throughout their history was that the Etruscans were of eastern origins, and they after all knew the Etruscans better than we do. By Roman times the Etruscans were routinely called Lydians in Latin poetry, and in the *Aeneid* Virgil talks of "Cerveteri, built on an ancient rock where once the Lydians, a race distinguished in war, settled the hills of Tuscany." The only writer in the ancient world who disagreed was Dionysius of Halicarnassus, a Greek historian writing at the time of Augustus, who claimed that the Etruscans were a race indigenous to Italy, mainly because he could find no resemblance between Etruscan language, religion and customs and those of the Lydia of his day.

Whatever modern archaeology may show, therefore, ancient authorities were agreed, with the exception of Dionysius, that the Etruscans came from the east. And even if the ancients did not always know best – we know far more than they did about the Mycenaeans, for example – the Etruscan language seems to confirm a connection outside Italy. As we shall see shortly, Etruscan is by no means as mysterious a language as popular opinion holds, and much progress has been made in interpreting its texts. All of this has served to confirm that without doubt Etruscan bears little relation to the other languages of Italy, the overwhelming majority of which belong to the Indo-European family; it is true that we do not know what language the Villanovans spoke, but if Etruscan culture was native to Italy we should expect to find some parallels with other languages spoken there during the Etruscan period. The problem would be solved, of course, if evidence for a language like Etruscan could be found in Lydia or elsewhere in the east, but so far this has not happened. On the other hand, inscriptions discovered on the island of Lemnos, off the northwest coast of Asia Minor, indicate that a language very similar to Etruscan was spoken there as late as the end of the 6th century BC. Is this a survival from a group of migrants who set off on a journey westwards, like those in Herodotus' story, stopped in Lemnos, and never left? Certainly it presents a strong challenge to those who deny the Etruscans' eastern origins, although it has been claimed that both the Lemnians and the Etruscans represent a survival from pre-Indo-European days in the Mediterranean, almost but not completely overwhelmed by the arrival of the Indo-European speakers sometime before 1000 BC.

And so since the time of Dionysius the argument has raged between the supporters of an eastern origin and the autochthonists; in the late 18th century a new theory credited the Etruscans with a northern origin, but this has found few supporters. It is probably safe to say that if either the eastern or autochthonous theory were capable of providing a generally convincing

Gold skyphos, or drinking cup, from the Bernardini Tomb at Praeneste, now in the Villa Giulia, Rome. It is about 48 cm high and dates to the mid-7th century. The shape is that of contemporary Greek pottery, but the addition of the sphinx ornaments above the handles is a typical piece of Etruscan elaboration.

Inscribed funerary stele from Kaminia on the island of Lemnos, now in the National Archaeological Museum, Athens. The language of the inscription is related to Etruscan, a fact which is regarded by many scholars as confirmation of Herodotus' theory of eastern origins.

Pair of ivory dice found in 1848 in a tomb at Tuscania. Bibliothèque Nationale, Paris. Although most scholars are agreed that the words on the faces signify the numbers one to six, there is wide disagreement as to which word represents each number.

and irrefutable body of evidence in its favor, the debate would have been over long ago. Significantly enough, however, both theories have their strong points: the autochthonists can point to a general line of continuous development in central Italy from the proto-Villanovans at the end of the Bronze Age to the Etruscans of the Orientalizing period, with no archaeological evidence for a major cultural break, while the easterners refuse to dismiss the opinions of the Etruscans' own contemporaries or overlook the correspondence between Etruscan and Lemnian. If, as seems likely, both sides are right in these arguments, the origin of the Etruscans is probably more complex than either side would admit, and recently scholars have begun to examine the question from a different point of view.

After all, one answer to the question "Who were the Etruscans?" is simply that Etruscan culture is first found in central Italy around 700 BC, where it developed, exerting immense political and artistic influence on Rome itself, until its decline and gradual absorption into the Roman world some 600 years later. Clearly many influences went to make it up, Villanovan, Greek, eastern, just as many cultures are the product of a wide range of outside influences. But it is important to remember that Etruscan culture as we know it existed solely in Italy: it has never been found outside the geographical area in which it developed. Few now accept literally Herodotus' story of a mass invasion of settlers from outside moving into a hitherto deserted central Italy, bringing their customs and goods with them, so that the problem now is not so much to identify the place from which the Etruscans came, but to sort out the forces which combined to form their culture; and even if the most visible of these is the Orientalizing element, we shall find many points in common between the Etruscans and their Italic neighbors.

The Etruscan language. In their language, however, the Etruscans had little in common with their neighbors or, except for the Lemnians, with anyone else. On the other hand, the popular reputations of Etruscan as an enigmatic undecipherable tongue does little justice to the slow but successful progress of research during the last 100 years, the difficulty of which has been largely due to the kind of inscriptions which have survived. Unlike the other languages of the ancient world, no Etruscan text has been passed down to us in manuscript form: we have no Etruscan history or literature, in fact only a dozen or so inscriptions of more than 20 words. The entire corpus of surviving Etruscan writing comes from finds in the course of excavations, and the overwhelming majority are only a few words long, either funeral epitaphs or dedications to a deity. They were carved or painted on funeral urns, walls, vases, small bronzes and other objects found in the tombs and repeat brief standard formulas, in the case of the epitaphs the name, parentage, age and rank of the dead, while the dedications give the name of the offerer and the deity involved. It is hardly surprising that Etruscan presents more problems than Greek or Latin; it is rather as if, in modern terms, a researcher with no knowledge of English were to try to understand its grammar or vocabulary from a study of the tombstones in the average country churchyard. In fact, all the surviving Etruscan inscriptions can be read (they are written in a form of the Greek alphabet) and many of them can be understood; what remains uncertain is the grammatical structure of the language and the linguistic family to which it belongs, and it is on these issues that research has concentrated.

The progress is a slow one. The 19th-century scholars' attempts to find a correspondence between Etruscan and other languages produced a mass of contradictory theories but little of value. Etruscan was compared with Latin, Greek and Hebrew, with Arabic and Chinese, with Ethiopian, Basque, Egyptian and Celtic, producing no results but much confusion; and in 1842 a German traveler in the Alps convinced himself that Etruscan was really a Teutonic language by finding Etruscan place names there: Vollgröss had started out as Velacarasa, he claimed, and Schleiss as Calusa.

The comparative technique, therefore, was little help, and the study and analysis of the structure of the inscriptions themselves, helped by the brevity and repetitive nature of the material, have proved much more successful. Since so many of them are funeral epitaphs their general significance is clear, and by comparing them it has been possible to identify some of the words. Many of the terms of kinship are now known – *clan* (son), *ati* (mother) and others – and also words like *avils* (years), although this method has not provided much help towards the understanding of Etruscan grammar. But with this basic vocabulary scholars have been able to approach the longer texts with encouraging results. The longest of all, the so-called Zagreb Mummy Text, is some 1,300 words long, and was originally a linen book (*liber linteus*) which during the Roman occupation of Egypt was torn into strips and used to wrap the mummified body of a woman. It was bought by a traveler in Egypt (its find place is unknown) and presented to the National Museum of Zagreb, where the inscription on the bindings was identified as Etruscan. Like so many other treasures it had been preserved by the dryness of the Egyptian climate, but we shall probably never know how an Etruscan sacred book – the text is a religious calendar – arrived in Egypt or why it was used in so strange a way. Clearly there must have been many similar books, and Etruscan urns often have stone or terracotta representations of their owners holding a scroll apparently made of linen or hide, or a pair of wooden tablets. But no originals have been found (they must have long since rotted away), and the other long inscriptions which have been preserved are on stone (including a boundary marker from Perugia), on metal or on clay; a clay tile inscribed with a funeral ritual was found at Capua.

These longer texts have enabled scholars to come to grips with the structure of Etruscan, and steady progress is being made in analyzing its workings. Although the language itself is not, as we have seen, related to the other languages of Italy, it was spoken and written by people in regular contact with the Romans, the Umbrians, and others whose religious and ritual texts are known to us. By comparing the structure of these to that of the Etruscan examples, it has been found that certain sacred formulas appear in both Etruscan and the other languages, and this has provided further help. But at the present stage the most valuable help of all would be the discovery of a "bilingual" text, with an Etruscan inscription and a translation in a known language – an Etruscan equivalent of the Rosetta stone. In 1964 a discovery was made at Pyrgi, one of the ports of ancient Cerveteri, which seemed to be just this. At this important site two temples have been excavated since work began there in 1957, and near the earlier one, built around 500 BC, were found three sheets of gold, neatly rolled up, together with bronze nails with gold heads; since the gold sheets have holes around their edges they were probably originally nailed to a wooden wall or door within the temple, and at a later time were removed and carefully buried nearby for protection. To the joy of the archaeologists, while two of these tablets bore Etruscan inscriptions, the third was in Phoenician (a

Above: One of the three gold plaques from Pyrgi, two of which are in Etruscan and the third in Phoenician. This one is the longer of the two Etruscan ones. Villa Giulia, Rome.

Above right: The Bocchoris vase, 23 cm high. Museo Nazionale, Tarquinia. Made of faience, it was produced, according to an inscription it bears, during the reign of the Egyptian King Bocchoris towards the end of the 8th century BC. It was found in a tomb at Tarquinia which dates to shortly after 700 BC, and is important both chronologically and for the light it throws on foreign contacts during the transitional period from Villanovan to Etruscan at Tarquinia.

Small impasto vase with archaic Etruscan inscription inside the body of a serpent, 6th century BC. Villa Giulia, Rome.

known language), apparently providing a translation of the longer Etruscan tablet and thereby the bilingual key which has been sought for so long. Unfortunately the translation is not a literal one but rather a paraphrase, and the Pyrgi tablets have not, as was at first hoped, solved all the remaining problems of Etruscan. Nonetheless, much has been learned from them, not only about the language, but about the Etruscans of Cerveteri and their Carthaginian neighbors: the inscriptions record the dedication by the ruler of Cerveteri of a temple to the Phoenician goddess Astarte, probably in honor of the alliance between the Etruscans and the Carthaginians which was formed in the middle of the 6th century BC against the Greeks.

Discoveries such as the Pyrgi tablets extend our knowledge of the Etruscan language, and at the same time provide written documentation for the course of Etruscan history. One of the results of a study of the language itself is, of course, that more information about a wide variety of aspects of Etruscan culture becomes available.

The rise of Etruscan power. The years immediately preceding the Etruscan alliance with Carthage have been described by one writer as "the golden centuries of Etruscan history"; and this seems an appropriate place to consider how the Etruscans reached such a position and how they fell from it.

Gold bracelets from the Regolini Galassi tomb, Cerveteri, 7th century BC. Vatican Museums. The sumptuous decoration was achieved by combining embossing with granulation, a technique which was probably eastern in origin but was perfected by the Etruscans. It consisted of soldering tiny granules of gold on to a flat surface.

The beginnings of Etruscan culture can be traced back to the end of the 8th century BC, when a number of cities near the coast, including Tarquinia, Veii and Cerveteri, began to show a new prosperity – just about the time that, to the north, the Este people were establishing their individual culture. The effects of this "Orientalizing" period are vividly illustrated by the contents of the tombs: the gold and silver of the Regolini Galassi tomb at Cerveteri and the Egyptian and Phoenician objects found in the Bocchoris tomb at Tarquinia are an indication of the sudden new wave of commercial success and the increase of contacts abroad which marked the late 8th and early 7th centuries BC. Much of this can be attributed to the arrival of the Greeks in Italy, bringing new ideas and opening up new markets, but the Etruscans' prosperity (and the growing urbanization which it produced) was founded on a solid commercial base, in the case of the southern cities the mineral resources of the nearby Tolfa mountains, rich in iron and copper. As in so many aspects of Etruscan culture, the continuity with the past is striking, since recent excavations have shown that as early as 1400 BC the Mycenaeans had established contacts in this part of central Italy. On the plateau of Luni the Swedish Institute at Rome has excavated a Bronze Age village, where the houses, instead of being the usual huts or caves, consisted of long communal dwellings (the largest is 42 meters long), and where Mycenaean pottery was found; the same area was later settled both by the Villanovans and by the Etruscans. In all periods the buildings were notable for their size and careful construction, although the valley of the Mignone where Luni lies is a wild and desolate region; and Apennine, Villanovan and Etruscan settlers were clearly attracted by the mineral riches of the Tolfa mountains nearby. In the same way during the 5th century BC the development of Etruscan cities further north was closely linked to their exploitation of the resources of Monte Amiata, Elba and the metalliferous hills of southern Tuscany.

But the southern cities were the first to establish themselves, and from their earliest days each one developed along its own individual lines. This process of separate development, which, as we have seen, is typical of Italy in the Iron Age, makes it difficult to generalize about Etruscan culture as a whole: each city had its own ways, and retained its own identity, in artistic styles, burial customs and probably social organization. Fortunately for the Romans this insistence on their individuality extended also to political issues, and it was the Etruscans' inability to act together against a common enemy which made possible Rome's systematic conquest of one city after another in the years following 390 BC. In the 7th century BC, however, Etruscan power was in the ascendant, and Etruscan ships controlled much of the western Mediterranean: their chief rivals, the Greeks, called them pirates in envy of their commercial successes, which were taking them as far west as Provence and Spain. Nearer home Elba, Corsica and Sardinia all fell under Etruscan control and by the end of the 7th century BC Rome itself was subject to Etruscan rule: according to Roman tradition Etruscan kings ruled there from 616 to 509 BC.

South of Rome, at Palestrina, the ancient city of Praeneste which had been founded by the Latins may have been ruled in the 7th century by Etruscan princes, judging from the contents of the tombs of some of the leading families which were discovered there in the 19th century. Even though the "excavators" of the last century were more concerned with collecting treasures than with scientific exploration, and much valuable information was thereby lost, the Praeneste tombs are of the greatest

Silver-gilt plate from the Bernardini Tomb, Praeneste, 7th century BC. Museo di Roma, Rome. The motifs are of the type known as Orientalizing, in this case Egyptian in style.

Caeretan *hydria* with the blinding of Polyphemus, c. 530 BC. Villa Giulia, Rome. Height 42 cm. It was probably painted by an east Greek artist working at Cerveteri.

importance for the Orientalizing period. Two of them, the Bernardini and Barberini tombs, contained grave goods of startling richness, among them gold jewelry and silver-gilt bowls which bear a strong resemblance to similar pieces found at Cerveteri. At both Praeneste and Cerveteri many of the objects show the influence of Egypt and the Near East, but seen through local eyes; and the presence of such elaborately Orientalizing pieces south of Rome is generally explained as the result of Etruscan domination there. Recent finds of a similar nature elsewhere in Latium, however, may suggest that Praeneste does not represent an island of Etruscan influence surrounded by independent Latin centers, but, in fact, is simply the most outstanding example of the effects of Orientalizing styles upon the Latins themselves, borrowed directly from the Greeks rather than imported by Etruscan overlords. Certainly it now seems that ideas of the kind were not limited to the Etruscans, and future excavations will probably do much to clarify the history of Latium in the 7th century BC, and the precise role played there by the Etruscans. The date of the tombs at Praeneste has been much discussed, but most of the material probably dates to 675–650 BC.

In the years following the Etruscan successes of the 7th century, the individual cities continued to develop their own artistic styles. Cerveteri was perhaps the most "international" of all. The Pyrgi tablets reveal cultural as well as political links with the Carthaginians, and in spite of trade rivalry Greek ideas were popular. Cerveteri was the only Etruscan city to

Above: The Boccanera plaques, three painted terracotta slabs from Cerveteri, c. 550 BC. British Museum. Height 73 cm. The left-hand side depicts the Judgment of Paris: Athene, dressed in a heavy red woolen robe, is followed by Hera and Aphrodite. To the right can be seen a procession of mourners.

Left: "Le Balze," Volterra, where erosion and landslides have carried away the hillside where the archaic necropolis probably lay.

have a treasury in the Sanctuary of Apollo at Delphi, and during the 6th century BC Caeretan *hydriai*, a type of Greek painted water jug found only at Cerveteri, were produced there by immigrant Greek craftsmen; their name is derived from Caere, the Latin form of Cerveteri. Sculptors at Cerveteri kept in close touch with developments in Ionia, and the famous double sarcophagus with husband and wife, versions of which are found in the Villa Giulia and in the Louvre, shows the influence of Greek ideas in the treatment of the faces and the drapery. The sense of immediacy and vividness is Etruscan, though, and so is the contrast between the fully modeled upper parts of the figures with their wonderfully expressive hands, and the schematic treatment of the legs which hardly seem to exist. Unlike his Greek contemporary, the Etruscan artist had little intellectual interest in how the body works or in unity of aesthetic expression.

A similar combination of Greek sophistication and Etruscan directness can be seen in the great series of statues from Veii which decorated the roof of a temple there at the end of the 6th century BC. Although the figure of Apollo is derived from Attic models, the almost brutal power of the god's smile and the tension of his pose recall the "primitive" nature of early Italic art.

While Cerveteri and Veii were notable for their sculpture, at Tarquinia there developed a school of painting which has left us, in the painted tombs of the 6th to 2nd centuries BC, one of the great collections of ancient art. Like other paintings found elsewhere in Italy during this period, including those in the tombs at Paestum which will be discussed in a later chapter, the Etruscan tomb paintings derived both stylistically and in subject matter from Greek models, but even more than in the case of the sculptures the models were adapted to Etruscan taste. The oldest of all these paintings, those in the Tomb of the Bulls of around 550 BC, include a scene from Greek mythology, the ambush of Troilus by Achilles, but the two heroic figures are overwhelmed by their surrounding, lost in a world of trees and plants; above this central panel are the bulls for which the tomb has been

named, and two erotic scenes – genuine Etruscan mysteries these, which have yet to be satisfactorily explained. A few years later, around 530–520 BC, the theme of the natural world and man's place in it was developed further in the Tomb of Hunting and Fishing, one of the most enchanting of all ancient masterpieces, where the brilliance of the colors is matched by the acuteness of observation.

Tarquinia, like Cerveteri, drew its wealth from trade, and even surpassed its rival in religious and political importance. The Etruscan kings of Rome were from Tarquinia, and the art of foretelling the future, so important in Etruscan religion, was first revealed there. According to a story retold by Cicero, a Tarquinian farmer was plowing his land when a divine child, Tages, rose from one of the furrows and taught the hastily assembled Etruscans the art of divination by reading the flight of birds and the entrails of animals; and even in Roman times, priests claiming to be Etruscan were in great demand as seers.

Meanwhile to the north, Chiusi and other northern cities, Volterra, Vetulonia, Arezzo and others, were also beginning to expand. For a number of reasons we know less about the early stages of their growth than about that of the southern cities. At Volterra, for example, the tombs of the 6th century were destroyed by a landslide which has left only the precipice known locally as "Le Balze," while Vetulonia seems to have been

Double sarcophagus from the Banditaccia necropolis, Cerveteri. Length 200 cm, height 140 cm. Late 6th century BC. Villa Giulia, Rome. The detailed and vivid modeling of the figures from the waist up is in strong contrast to the summary treatment of the lower parts of the bodies.

abandoned entirely between the 6th and 3rd centuries. Other cities like Arezzo and Cortona did not really begin to develop before the 5th century BC. Chiusi itself, however, although more isolated than the coastal cities and dependent for its prosperity on agriculture rather than trade, was clearly affected from a relatively earlier period by ideas from abroad. Large numbers of Greek vases were imported, including the famous François vase, and stone relief carvings showing eastern influences were produced locally. The earliest painted tombs (now, alas, disappeared) were even earlier in date than those at Tarquinia. The most characteristic products of Chiusi and the towns in its territory are the so-called "canopic" urns, ash urns crowned with the model of a human head, and with bodies that often have human features, which seem a natural outgrowth of the Villanovan helmet-urns. There has been much argument as to whether the heads represent portraits of the deceased, and thereby foreshadow the Roman tradition of ancestor busts, or are merely stylized after Greek models. In favor of the former is the pronounced individuality that many of them suggest, in spite of their obvious simplicity and crudeness of manufacture.

By the end of the 6th century BC Etruscan power had reached its height. The Etruscans had crossed the Apennines and taken over Bologna, as we have seen, and from the Po valley to Campania Italy was under their influence. Only the east coast remained independent, and the Tiber formed a natural boundary which protected the Umbrians and the other Italic tribes who lived there. Outside Italy the Etruscans were trading throughout the Mediterranean, and in 540 BC combined with the Carthaginians to oust the Greeks from Corsica. But the price paid for the victory over the Greeks was a Carthaginian presence in Sardinia, which severely limited the possibilities of Etruscan expansion, and shortly afterwards the Etruscans lost their control of Latium and Campania: in 509 BC the Etruscan kings were driven out of Rome, and in 474 the Syracusans

Above: Canopic urn from Chiusi, 6th century BC. Museo Civico, Chiusi. The element of portraiture in this example is very rudimentary, but the maker has taken care to indicate the sex of the figure, and presumably of the urn's occupant.

Above left: The François vase. Detail showing the hunting of the Calydonian boar and, below, the chariot race at the funeral games of Patroclus. Note the labels which serve to identify the figures.

Left: Canopic urn from Chiusi, 7th–6th century BC. Museo Etrusco, Chiusi. The terracotta urn sits on a bronze "throne." Note the hairstyle, which is very similar to that of contemporary Greek sculpture.

destroyed an Etruscan fleet off Cumae and by establishing a garrison on Ischia cut the Etruscans off from southern Italy and Sicily. One of the effects of this was to leave Campania open to the Samnites, whom we shall meet in the next chapter. The 5th century BC was, therefore, one of retrenchment, and the Etruscans never again recovered their lost territories. But while the initial setbacks had been caused by foreign rivals, the Greeks and Carthaginians, in Italy a far more ominous threat was developing in the growing power of Rome, and the danger was compounded by the inability (or unwillingness) of the individual Etruscan cities to unite. Although there existed a loose federation of the 12 principal Etruscan cities, the "dodecapolis" referred to by ancient writers, the chief purpose of this league was to organize and hold religious festivals and games. These "pan-Etruscan" meetings took place annually at a sanctuary known as the Fanum Voltumnae, in the territory of Volsinii near Lake Bolsena; the sanctuary itself has never been discovered, and even the location of the city of Volsinii is uncertain, some scholars identifying it with Orvieto and others with the Etruscan settlement recently excavated at Bolsena. It seems unlikely that the meetings produced any political unity, and the leading cities retained their independence to act in what they thought to be their own interest. When, therefore, in 396 BC the Romans concluded a ten-year siege of Veii with the total destruction of the city, they could rely on the non-interference of the other Etruscan cities, including Veii's nearest neighbor, Cerveteri. The invasion of Italy by the Gauls in 390 BC only postponed a similar fate for the other southern cities, and although Rome itself was sacked, its quick recovery and reconstruction were followed by further moves against the Etruscans. Tarquinia was subdued by 351 BC, two years after Cerveteri had signed a peace treaty which saved it from destruction but placed it firmly on the Roman side; the Caeretans had always been friendly to Rome, and the treaty (and their consequent non-intervention) left the Romans free to deal with Tarquinia.

The collapse of the Etruscan world. The increasing collapse of Etruscan power and the grim future awaiting those Etruscan cities which still remained free are forcefully expressed in the frescoes of the François tomb at Vulci. Although Vulci was not finally conquered until 280 BC, these paintings, commissioned in the middle of the 4th century BC by one of its leading families, fully express the violence and anxiety of the times. In the antechamber is the portrait of the tomb's owner, Vel Saties, one of the most moving of all Etruscan works of art: accompanied by his slave, Arnza (the figures are named in the inscriptions), he moves solemnly and in deep thought towards the next life. The inner chamber is decorated with scenes of battle: Etruscans fight with Romans and, significantly, with other Etruscans. On one wall is the most overwhelming of all visions of the collapse of the Etruscan world. The scene is drawn from Greek mythology, the sacrifice of Trojan prisoners, but the message is an immediate one. One of the prisoners stands, his hands bound behind him, forced to watch the decapitation of his comrade, and to either side of the central scene of execution are the two Etruscan deities of death. The demon Charun, armed with a hammer, represents the horror and violence of death, his face composed of putrefying flesh which decays before our eyes, and he is accompanied by the goddess Vanth, symbol of the implacability of fate who stands watching the scene with a cold indifference which seems even more terrifying that Charun's brutality. With their world collapsing around them, such visions can have brought the Etruscans little comfort as they faced death, and by now their vision of the next world was of a place without hope, ruled over by demons and monsters, where the troubles of this life were followed by the tortures of the next. An elaborate tomb at Tarquinia, the Tomb of Orcus, was painted at different times during the 4th century BC with scenes of life in the underworld which mingle heroes and demons in the gloom.

The great Etruscan centers of southern Tuscany and Latium were, as the natural rivals of Rome, inevitably the earliest to be conquered, but during the 3rd and 2nd centuries BC the northern cities continued to prosper, and in some cases to expand, although the price paid was cooperation with Rome. When the Romans under Scipio mounted an expedition against Carthage in 205 BC, Volterra contributed fittings for the ships, wood for their keels and a large quantity of grain, while Populonia provided iron and Arezzo helmets and weapons. Nonetheless, Volterra, for one, retained its independence and continued to mint its own coinage. The city expanded and new buildings were added, and much of the valley of the river Elsa to the east fell under its control. Under a prosperity derived from agriculture rather than commerce, art flourished, and Volterran bronzes, painted vases and carved alabaster funeral urns were produced in large quantities both for home consumption and for export. Arezzo, too, developed an artistic tradition: the famous Chimaera was probably made at the end of the 5th century BC, and a fine series of architectural terracottas have been found which date to the 3rd and 2nd centuries.

In general the prevailing artistic influence throughout the last centuries of Etruscan history remained a Greek one and, although individual cities retained their special interests and character, local differences are less noticeable. The last great Etruscan achievement in the arts, this common artistic language is found not only in central Italy, but, as we shall see, was also shared with southern Italy, affecting in the process the art of Rome. The relationship between Roman and Etruscan art is a complex one, involving cultural exchanges in both directions, but without doubt works like the statue of Aulus Metellus, known as the "Orator," prefigure both in gesture and in portrait much of Roman imperial sculpture. This last great work of Etruscan art comes from the beginning of the 1st century BC, immediately preceding the final collapse of Etruscan culture, when the magistrate whom the statue represents could still be identified by an inscription in Etruscan. Perhaps within his lifetime Roman control of Italy, and Roman political domination of both her Italic and her Etruscan neighbors, produced in 91 BC one last challenge to her authority. Etruscans, Samnites and others united in what is called the Social War (the war begun by Rome's allies or *socii*) in an attempt to gain their freedom. But it was too late, and by 88 BC the cities which had revolted were reduced to the status of Roman *coloniae* and settled by Roman veterans. Individual families, in the following centuries, could boast of Etruscan ancestry and even claim to speak Etruscan, but Etruscan culture was dead.

Recent discoveries. There is almost no aspect of Etruscan culture in which some new advance has not been made in the last few years. We have seen something of the progress in the understanding of Etruscan inscriptions, and in other areas too – religion, architecture, politics, history – new information is being discovered and old information reexamined. Most of this progress is the result of new excavations, but in some cases a

Fresco from the François tomb, Vulci, 3rd century BC. Now in the Torlonia collection, Villa Albani, Rome. The episode shown here is the execution of Trojan prisoners.

more rounded picture of Etruscan life is being produced by asking questions about matters other than where the Etruscans came from or what language they spoke. How, for example, did the Etruscans dress? Professor Larissa Bonfante has recently provided a number of answers in a book which examines the evidence provided by their art, and compares Etruscan dress with that of the Greeks. For the most part Etruscan taste is more fussy and at the same time more realistic than the Greek, and the general picture which emerges is of a people devoted to elaborate decoration, and an upper class with the leisure to spend on self-adornment.

New excavations are, of course, the most exciting way of acquiring new information, and this is especially true in the case of the Etruscans. Their obsession with death and the construction of tombs, and the obsession of their discoverers in the 19th and early 20th centuries with the treasures found in the tombs, has meant that until recently much more was known about Etruscan funerary customs than about their way of life. The majority of finds still come from tombs, but the balance is being corrected. The Swedish Institute at Rome has excavated an Etruscan town at Acquarossa near Viterbo, which was first settled at the beginning of the 7th century BC, destroyed around 500 BC, and subsequently abandoned. Most Etruscan cities were either rebuilt by the Romans, like Fiesole and Perugia, or completely destroyed by them, like Veii. At Acquarossa, untouched since the 5th century BC, the excavators have found immensely valuable evidence for Etruscan architecture and town planning during their golden years: as well as foundations, numerous terracotta plaques and decorations were preserved, the most recent of which dates to the years immediately before the town's destruction.

Little is known about Etruscan temples or sanctuaries, and the

Bronze striding warrior armed with a lance. Museo Archeologico, Perugia.

Opposite: Bronze figurine from Populonia showing the suicide of Ajax, c. 490 BC. Museo Archeologico, Florence. Height 8·5 cm. One of the very finest of Etruscan bronzes, this originally formed part of a larger object, now lost.

excavation of a 6th-century building complex which seems to be a sanctuary at Murlo, to the south of Siena, is perhaps the most important of all recent discoveries, both for the information it provides on Etruscan religion and for the superb quality of the finds themselves. The excavations, under the direction of Kyle M. Phillips jr., have uncovered a series of structures built around 575 BC over an earlier building which had been destroyed by fire shortly after 600 BC. For the moment the most puzzling aspect of the sanctuary is the fact that around 525 BC it was completely destroyed, apparently deliberately, and never used again. Possibly the destructions of both Murlo and Acquarossa are related to the disturbances affecting the Etruscan world as a whole at the end of the 6th century, although they may be the result of the expansion of nearby centers – in the case of Murlo, that of Chiusi. The most spectacular finds come from the sanctuary building itself. Like the temple of Apollo at Veii, the roof of the building was covered with life-sized terracotta figures, and parts of 13 of them have survived. These statues, and numerous terracotta relief plaques with scenes of banqueting, processions and horse racing, suggest a very high artistic level for a relatively inaccessible region, a long way from any of the great centers, and show vividly how Etruscan culture, far from being isolated, had contacts elsewhere in Italy throughout the 6th century. The broad-brimmed hats and pointed shoes of the Murlo figures can be found to the north on the situlae of the Este people, and a parallel with the Picenes, a tribe related to the Umbrians who lived across the Tiber to the east, is provided by the broad rim of the helmet of the famous Capestrano warrior. It will take a long time before the significance of the finds from Murlo has been finally absorbed, but they have already made a profound impression on the study of the Etruscans, not least because of the speed and exemplary care with which they have been published and made available to the academic community. As a result scholars are able to make their own assessments of the discoveries and, indeed, of the nature of the site itself. It has recently been suggested, for example, that Murlo was a secular rather than sacred building complex, the home perhaps of a local ruler; and although this remains a minority view, the debate will certainly continue.

No less exciting and informative has been the discovery of the port of Tarquinia at Gravisca. Near the modern seaside resort of Porto Clementino, although nothing was visible on the surface, aerial photography had revealed the town plan of a Roman colony, and in 1969 excavation was begun. It soon became clear that not only the remains of the Roman town were buried there, but also an earlier Etruscan one, whose origins go back to the early 6th century BC. A number of buildings have been uncovered, but the most startling find has been of a Greek colony on the edge of the Etruscan town, founded around 600 BC and abandoned about 480 BC. Wells, houses and a sanctuary have come to light; the sanctuary was dedicated to Hera and Aphrodite, and numbers of vases have been found inscribed in Greek with dedications to them. For the first time, therefore, evidence has been found of an actual Greek community living alongside an Etruscan one, influencing Etruscan art and trading with them – presumably the colony was one of merchants and shippers – while continuing to worship their own gods. We can even identify more precisely one of the Greek traders, by means of an inscribed dedication on a stone anchor, the first Greek stone inscription ever to have been found in an Etruscan context. The name of its donor is Sostratus of Aegina, and a passage in Herodotus refers to a certain Sostratus of Aegina, son of

Laodamas, as a merchant whose success in his trade with Spain was unequaled by any rival. Apparently Sostratus used Tarquinia's port as a stopping-off place on his way west.

The last ten years alone, therefore, have produced a wealth of new discoveries and work at these and other sites is still continuing. As new evidence is found for Etruscan culture in all its aspects, a picture is slowly emerging of a society distinctive and characteristic on the one hand, but at the same time intimately linked to the cultures surrounding it. The most prominent influence, as we have seen, is Greek, but at the same time the Etruscans also came into contact with their Italian neighbors and we can see something of the effects of this by taking a brief look at the Italic tribes to their east.

The Umbrians and the Picenes. By the end of the 7th century BC, while the Etruscans were at the height of their power, a number of Italic peoples had established themselves in central and southern Italy. Some of these, like the Faliscans to the north of Rome, developed a culture very similar to the Etruscans, and their geographical proximity to the great Etruscan centers obviously facilitated cultural exchange. In the more remote regions, however, a more independent life-style developed, and although most of these Italic tribes spoke languages belonging to a general group known as Umbro-Sabellian, regional variations can be found in their culture. The Umbrians, who have given their name to the province of Italy still called Umbria, settled in the area between Gubbio and Todi. During the 6th

Terracotta head of Hermes from the Portonaccio sanctuary at Veii, late 6th or early 5th century BC. Villa Giulia, Rome. Height 34 cm. It formed part of a full-length statue of the god which, together with the Apollo and other statues, decorated the ridge of the temple roof in the sanctuary.

century BC, while their contacts with the Etruscans were relatively casual, they lived in small settlements, retaining the primitive life-style and customs of a century earlier. Even when Etruscan expansion brought the Umbrians into closer contact with their more civilized western neighbors they did not lose their cultural independence, and it was not until Rome's unification of the entire peninsula that they became drawn into the mainstream of Italian life. As late as the end of the 3rd century BC they were still using their own language, Umbrian, as is shown by the seven inscribed bronze tablets, the so-called Eugubian tables, found at Gubbio in 1444, near the Roman theater there. The tablets show that the Umbrians clearly had much in common with both the Etruscans and the Latins: five of the tablets are written in Etruscan characters and two in Latin letters, and the inscriptions seem to use religious formulas which are similar to those on the Zagreb Mummy Text and early Roman sacred texts, some of which were preserved by later Roman writers like Cato. On the other hand, in spite of many similarities to Latin, the Umbrian language is still different not only from Etruscan but from the other Umbro-Sabellian languages to which it is related, different enough in fact to prevent complete understanding of the texts.

The same mixed influences can be found in the most famous sculpture to come from ancient Umbria, the "Mars of Todi," which was found at Todi and is now in the Vatican Museum. Here the technical finish is Etruscan in quality, but the style shows a typically Italic conservatism: although the statue was made at the end of the 4th or beginning of the 3rd century BC, the influence is that of Greek sculpture of a century earlier. It was probably made by a local craftsman who had studied with an Etruscan master; even if it is actually of Etruscan manufacture it was clearly intended for a local purchaser, and the breastplate is inscribed in Umbrian with the name of its owner, Ahal Trutitis.

The Umbrians are only one of the Italic peoples who managed to be influenced but not absorbed by the Etruscans. Further east were the Picenes, affected not only by the Etruscans and Greeks but also by the Este people, yet retaining their own local characteristics, a conservative warrior tribe whose art, though less sophisticated than the Etruscans', is still capable of considerable expression. The clay vase handle in the form of a human figure found in recent excavations at Campovalano belongs to the same tradition of geometric abstraction which is found in Villanovan art, although it comes from sometime later than the Villanovan examples, and shows a remarkable beauty and elegance of form. Less elegant, but even more powerful, is the stone head of a warrior from Numana and most impressive of all the great statue of a warrior from Capestrano. The figure was originally placed over a tomb, probably as a representation of the dead man who stands, supported by two props and in full armor, guarding his grave and his land. He recalls the story of Polybius, the Greek historian, who tells how the bodies of some of the most noble of Romans were placed standing upright, after their death, in the Roman Forum to remind the citizens of their glorious deeds. The contrasts between the massive scale of the figure and the small head, the sinuous, almost graceful body and the weapons that he carries, and the monumentality of the figure as a whole, combine to produce an overwhelming work, and one very different from the mainstream of Etruscan-inspired Italic art. Like the Umbrians, the Picenes were able, even in the cultural confusion of 6th-century Italy, to keep their independence.

Mars of Todi. Umbrian bronze of the early 4th century BC. Vatican Museums. Height 123 cm. Both the lance, which was originally in the right hand, and the helmet are now lost. An inscription in Umbrian is incised on the corselet.

The Painted Tombs of Tarquinia

The 150 or so painted tombs discovered so far at Tarquinia provide invaluable information about Etruscan life and religion, quite apart from the light they throw on the history of ancient painting. Most of them were executed in the same way: a coat of plaster was applied to the walls of the tomb, and a quick sketch was often made with a sharp point to provide a guide for the painter. The colors themselves were vegetable and mineral based, and were applied while the plaster was still wet to fix them. Most of the tombs consist of a single chamber (the Tomb of the Bulls is an exception), and date from the mid-6th to the mid-5th century BC. Later ones, like the Tomb of Orcus, are larger and more complex in plan.

1 Tomb of the Leopards, mid-5th century BC. Many of the tombs of this period show scenes of the banqueting which formed part of the funeral ceremonies. During the feasts the diners were entertained by music and dancing, and the right-hand wall of this tomb shows two musicians, a lyre player and a flautist who is playing a double flute. Note the drinking cup in the hand of the figure on the left: it is a painted version of the typically Etruscan black ware known as *bucchero*.

2 Tomb of the Triclinium, c. 470 BC. The subject matter of these paintings is very similar to that of the Tomb of the Leopards. On the end wall (here on the right) we see the banqueters reclining on couches and waited on by servants; above them funerary wreaths are painted to give the impression of being suspended from the walls. The long side wall is filled with the figures of dancers and musicians; the roof, like that of the Tomb of the Leopards, is decorated with a checkerboard design. The fineness of line and delicate coloring, however, suggest an artist more familiar with Greek models.

3, 4 and 5 Tomb of Hunting and Fishing, c. 520 BC. Although badly damaged in places, the paintings convey a wonderful sense of light and air: the bluish haze seems to evoke all the sensations of sea and spray. Both men and animals are rendered naturalistically, with some particularly acute pieces of observation: notice the bird perched on the waves just to the left of the boat. The wide range of colors and the variety of movement all enhance the general effect. Elsewhere in the tomb the preparations for the funeral feast are shown. While the servant girl on the left prepares the funeral garlands (some of

1

2

3

4

5

6

7

8

which are painted as if hanging on the wall), the central couple is serenaded. Note the woman's elaborate headdress and earrings, and the rather ambiguous position of her companion's legs.

6 Terracotta winged horses from the temple at Tarquinia known as the Ara della Regina, 4th–3rd century BC. Height 115 cm. The slab on which these horses are modeled in relief originally covered the left-hand side of the end of the central roof beam. To the right was the chariot which the horses were drawing, with a goddess standing in it. She presumably represented the patron deity of the temple, although not enough of the figure has survived to permit an identification. The horses themselves, with their combination of naturalism and imagination, are among the marvels of Etruscan art.

7, 8 and 11 Tomb of the Bulls, second half of the 6th century BC. This is the only tomb to be decorated with a mythological subject, the ambush of Troilus by Achilles during the Trojan War. The theme is Greek, but the treatment is Etruscan, with the figures almost lost among the trees and plants, and a gently plashing fountain. The figure of Troilus on his spirited horse is characteristically elongated, and wears the typical pointed Etruscan shoes. But the tomb is named for the two strange episodes in the band above. To the left a bull sits with its back turned to an erotic scene involving two men and a girl; to the right a bearded bull with erect phallus charges towards a man in a blond wig engaging in homosexual activity with a youth. Do these groups imply a condemnation of homosexuality, with the charging bull attacking the two male figures while the other one ignores the "normal" couple? Are they related to a fertility cult? Were they, indeed, painted at the same time as the rest of the tomb? So far scholars have failed to agree.

9 and 10 The Tomb of Orcus was first constructed in the mid-4th century, and subsequently enlarged. Its subjects reflect the increasing gloom that was becoming characteristic of Etruscan art during the centuries of gradual defeat at the hands of the Romans, in contrast to the mood of relaxed confidence of the earlier periods. The bearded male profile represents Hades himself, as the inscription tells us, the god of the underworld. The other figure is of a noble Etruscan lady named Velia. She stares into the darkness, somberly but with dignity, richly attired in elaborately worked earrings and necklaces. The realistic depiction of the eye, shown from the side rather than frontally as in the earlier period, is a clear indication of the artist's knowledge of late 4th-century BC Greek models.

9

10

11

5 SOUTH OF ROME

In contrast to the relatively homogeneous cultural patterns of north and central Italy, where a dominant culture can generally be recognized in each geographical area, the picture presented by southern Italy is a much more confused one. Not only is the number of distinct cultural groups greater, and their history and development difficult to follow, but it is often hard to be certain whether we are dealing with genuinely different cultures or merely branches of a single group. Nor is the situation made easier by the effects of Greek colonization there. We have seen that the arrival of the Greeks in the 8th century BC marked a major stage in the development of early Italy, the results of which were felt throughout the entire peninsula: the newly discovered Greek settlement at Gravisca near Tarquinia, described in the previous chapter, is an example of Greek social and economic interpenetration of an already existing society. In the case of the Etruscans, themselves a sophisticated and developed people, the result of contact with the Greeks was strong enough; it is not surprising therefore that the impact of the Greek colonies on southern Italy, the chief area of Greek expansion, was so much more powerful, since in general the native population was technologically and culturally so much less developed. The effects of Greek ideas, ranging from religion to artistic styles to the alphabet, often make it difficult for us to perceive the native characteristics of the peoples who willingly or unwillingly succumbed to these foreign influences, particularly since, in addition to the Greeks, the Etruscans also aimed for that political and economic domination of southern Italy which after the succeeding centuries the Romans finally achieved. The Greek cities of Italy and Sicily are, of course, of major importance in the history of the ancient world and the development of western civilization; and we shall look at them briefly at the end of this chapter. For the moment, however, we must try to see beneath the veneer of Hellenic culture to the Italic origins of the peoples whom the Greeks found already established in Italy when they arrived there. Our evidence is from a variety of sources: in addition to the archaeological material, much of it of recent discovery, the few surviving inscriptions give some indication of linguistic and racial patterns, and the traditions and stories preserved by later Roman historians are at times helpful, although naturally frequently biased in the Romans' favor.

In general, and at the risk of oversimplification, the chief Italic tribes and their areas of influence seem to have been as follows. To the north and east of Rome lay the territory of the Umbrians, whom we have already met, with their centers at Gubbio, Todi and elsewhere. Nearer to Rome, in Latium itself were the Volscians and the Sabines, both among Rome's bitterest enemies, while in the south of Latium a number of smaller but equally belligerent peoples had settled, including the Aequi, the Marsi and

Samnite warrior from a tomb painting at
Paestum. 4th century BC.

the Vestini. In Campania the situation was more complex. The first Italic people to establish settlements there were the Oscans, who existed in relative peace during the 7th and 6th centuries BC alongside the newly arrived Greeks, although that peace was disturbed during the 6th century BC by the incursions of Etruscan merchants and colonists from further north. At the end of the 5th century BC another Italic tribe, the Samnites, moved southward from their territories in the mountains of central Italy, conquering and occupying the cities which had been founded by Oscans, Greeks and Etruscans. Their possession of Campania provided the Samnites with a base of activities against Rome, and as late as the 1st century BC they led the attack on Rome by her Italian "allies" in the Social War of 90–88 BC. Samnite control also spread southwards, and the Italic peoples who had settled in what are now Basilicata and Calabria, the Lucanians and the Bruttians, fell under their influence during the 4th century BC.

It is important to remember that all these peoples, in spite of their common characteristics, thought of themselves as separate: there is no

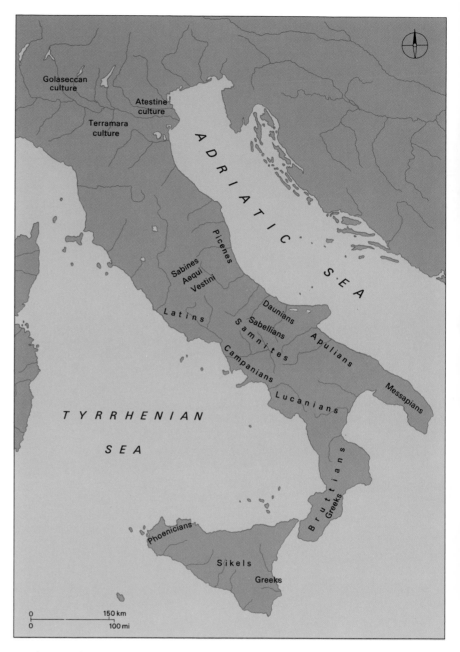

The main patterns of cultural distribution in Italy.

evidence of any strong feeling of Italic unity among the various tribes, nor was there any move to form a confederation. Indeed for the most part their dealings with one another were hostile, and only under the threat of Roman domination did they make any attempt to act together. Even then their efforts were only partial and of course unsuccessful: if the Romans had had to face a unified Italic opposition to their expansion, the history of the last 2,000 years might have been very different. But in spite of their apparent individuality these various tribes must have shared a common origin. Although their languages have certain local differences, they all belong to a single family, known generally as either Osco-Umbrian or Umbro-Sabellian. (The confusion of terminology is unfortunate: Sabellian is used as the name of the linguistic family itself, with Umbrian and Oscan as regional variations. But these three terms, Sabellian, Oscan and Umbrian, can also be used for the individual tribes themselves, while Osco-Umbrian and Umbro-Sabellian are applied only to the language group. As a further complication Sabellian, as applied to the people rather than the language, is sometimes used as a collective term for a number of Italic tribes, and sometimes as an alternative form of Samnite, to which it is philologically related.) The languages of this family are Indo-European in origin, and yet show marked differences from Latin, also an Indo-European tongue. In addition to the linguistic bond, the Italic peoples had a number of customs and traditions in common, the best-known of which is the *ver sacrum* or sacred spring: in certain years children born in the spring were dedicated to a deity, and when they came of age were required to leave their home territory and found a new center elsewhere. Whether these mass migrations were a means to avoid overpopulation – or rather overexploitation of meager agricultural resources – or whether they were a deliberate method of colonization remains uncertain; what is significant is that they were characteristic of a wide range of Italic peoples and resulted in the spread of Italic culture over most of central and southern Italy.

What were the origins of this basic cultural unity, of which the separate tribes seemed themselves so unaware? Like most aspects of early Italy the subject has been hotly debated, but it is surely no coincidence that the geographical area of Italic civilization corresponds to a remarkable degree with that of the Apennine culture of the Middle and Late Bronze Age, itself notably uniform. The Italic peoples may have been the direct descendants of their Apennine forebears, protected from many of the effects of foreign immigration by the remoteness of their settlements; or alternatively, new arrivals in eastern and southern Italy may have inherited the cultural stability of the Apennine period, while introducing their own language and customs. The difficulty is, as so often, to decide when an Indo-European language was introduced into Italy, and by whom, and it is not made any easier by the fact that although the Umbro-Sabellian and the Latin families of language are both of Indo-European origin and have much in common, they are not the same. But in either case the existence of a basic Italic cultural unity cannot be disputed, and even the lack of political unity or the effects of Greek, Etruscan or Roman ideas do not conceal it.

In addition to the Italic tribes of central and southern Italy there are a number of peoples in eastern Italy who seem generally connected with their Italic neighbors, but whose cultures show special features of their own: they include the Picenes, whom we have already seen, and the Daunians, Peucetians and Messapians of Apulia. Before taking a look at the Apulians, however, we should examine in more detail the most formidable of the Italic peoples, the Samnites, particularly since in doing so we shall meet many of the other groups active in southern Italy.

The Samnites. If it is true that environment is a major force in creating a people's character, the hardy, rugged Samnites may well have been formed by their original home, the wild mountains of central Italy. We still know very little about the early stages of their history, but from the beginning their interests seem to have been military, and some magnificent examples of bronze armor have been found at the Samnite town of Aufidena, known today as Alfedena. But in their search for new territories to conquer and occupy, these warrior tribesmen were inevitably hindered by the presence of other peoples, often more sophisticated and better equipped. Throughout the 7th and 6th centuries, for example, the Etruscans maintained a firm hold on much of central Italy, and had even established bases in Campania, where they founded the city of Capua.

Nonetheless it was Campania that attracted the Samnites' attention, with its rich farm land and strategically valuable coast, and their conquest of it was made possible, ironically enough, by a third group of colonizers, the Greeks. It was the Greeks, after all, who had been the first foreigners to settle there when in the 8th century BC Euboeans had founded the colonies of Pithecoussae and Cuma. In the years following, Greek influence continued to spread, and the Greek colonizers seem to have managed to coexist peacefully with the native Italic population, the Oscans. The tranquillity and cultural interchange of this period are vividly illustrated by the early history of Pompeii, a city that has provided us with so much information about later Roman culture, and which was probably founded by the Oscans at the beginning of the 7th century BC. The Greek traders and settlers of this period, although primarily interested in developing good commercial relations with their neighbors, could not fail at the same time to make a strong impact on the less developed culture of the Italic communities, and at Pompeii two sanctuaries of the 6th century BC have been found, one dedicated to Apollo and the other to Herakles, which show the strength of Greek influence. So pronounced is this that some scholars have suggested that Pompeii may actually have been a Greek colony from the beginning, and even if Pompeii's origins were Oscan, it soon formed part of an area which was becoming increasingly Hellenized as other Greek cities were founded throughout southern Italy.

But meanwhile to the north the spread of Etruscan power had brought Rome itself into Etruscan hands, and by the 6th century, if not earlier, Etruscan trade with the Greek and Oscan cities of Campania had developed into conquest and occupation. New Etruscan cities, including Capua, were founded, and in spite of fierce Greek opposition, for a time the Etruscans established a marked commercial superiority. But in 524 BC an Etruscan attack on Cumae, still one of the most powerful Greek cities, was unsuccessful and a few years later the expulsion of the Etruscan rulers of Rome further weakened the Etruscans in Campania by cutting off their communications with the north. By the end of the 6th century BC the Etruscans were trapped between the Latins to the north and the Greeks to the south and west, and their old enemies the Cumaeans in alliance with forces from the Greek city of Syracuse, themselves buoyed by their recent triumph over an attempted Carthaginian invasion of Sicily, finally defeated the Etruscans in 474 BC in a decisive naval battle off Cumae. Now the Greeks could reestablish their control in southern Italy and Sicily, and relax – or so they thought. The mood of hope is perfectly caught in an ode by Pindar, the great Greek lyric poet: "Zeus, son of Cronus, grant, I beg you, that the Carthaginians and the Etruscans with their war cries may now stay quietly at home, in view of the disastrous fate their pride brought on their ships at Cumae and their sufferings at the hands of the ruler of Syracuse." Not for a moment would it have occurred to Pindar or his contemporaries that the next challenge to Greek control of southern Italy, this time a successful one, would come not from either Carthage or Etruria, but from an uncivilized Italic mountain tribe.

Civilized or not, the Samnites had the sense to see that the defeat of the Etruscans left a temporary vacuum, and they were quick to seize their opportunity. Capua, the one remaining Etruscan stronghold, may have been conquered as early as 438 BC, and by 421 BC Cumae had also fallen; by the end of the 5th century BC almost the entire coast from Cumae to Paestum was in Samnite hands, as well as much of the interior of Campania. Once again Pompeii provides valuable evidence for the history of this period.

Right: Samnite bronze armor (breastplate and belt) from the tomb of a warrior in the cemetery at Alfedena, in the central region of the Abruzzi. National Museum of Wales, Howard de Walden collection (on loan to Ashmolean Museum, Oxford).

Below: Samnite capital from Pompeii, 3rd century BC. Antiquarium, Pompeii. Although the figured capital is Hellenistic in origin, its treatment in this case is far from Greek. The vigor of the ornamentation, with its rough textures and abrupt transitions, hides the shape of the capital itself.

Like its neighbors it had undergone a period of Etruscan influence and possibly occupation; now the Samnites attacked and occupied it, and many traces remain of their subsequent rebuilding. For the first time since its original foundation by the Oscans Pompeii became again an Italic city, and a number of houses from the Samnite period have survived, as well as a palaestra, or gymnasium. But although the Samnites had demonstrated their military superiority, they could not avoid being influenced by the cultures which they had defeated. The Roman historian Livy, describing the impact of Greek ideas on their Roman conquerors, remarked that in defeat the Greeks took captive their very captors by the cultural influence which they continued to exert; and the same might be observed of the marked Greek characteristics of the Samnite centers which developed in southern Italy. It is perhaps fairer, though, to say that both Romans and Samnites had the good sense to take over the most attractive aspects of the culture of their victims, while still retaining their own strengths.

Something of this cultural mixing can be seen in a small sanctuary discovered in 1947 just outside the walls of Pompeii, on the hill of Sant'Abbondio. The shrine was dedicated to Dionysus, and remained in use from its construction during the Samnite period of occupation until the destruction of Roman Pompeii by the eruption of Vesuvius in 79 AD. The cult of Dionysus was, of course, Greek in origin, and the figures represented on the pediment are familiar from Greek mythology, Dionysus himself, Ariadne, Eros, a Silenus, but the style of the sculpture is Italic, and an inscription in Oscan on the altar tells us that it had been dedicated by Maras Atiniis, the Samnite aedile of the town. In this way Greek ideas and themes were adopted by their conquerors, but became assimilated to local ways and adapted to local tastes. That this is just not an isolated example is proved by a sculptured metope found in Pompeii itself, which shows an episode from Greek mythology in which Ixion is nailed to a wheel by Hephaestus in the presence of Athene; once again, however, the figures are treated in a

Diving figures from the Tomb of the Diver, Paestum (*above*), c. 470 BC, and the Tomb of Hunting and Fishing, Tarquinia (*opposite*), c. 520 BC. The painting from Paestum is more stylized, less exuberant (notice the decorative palmettes on the right), but both show the same sensitivity to space and light.

thoroughly Italic way, and Athene herself, the virgin warrior goddess of Greek tradition, holds the tools with the aid of which Ixion is to be fastened to the wheel for all the world as if she were some local Campanian carpenter. If the concept is Greek, the execution is Italic.

But the most vivid illustrations of the relationship that was to develop between Greek and Italic culture come from further south in Campania, where the Greek colony of Poseidonia, better known to us by its Roman name of Paestum, was conquered around 400 BC by the Lucanians, an Italic tribe increasingly subject to Samnite domination. Poseidonia had been founded at the end of the 7th century BC by another Greek city of southern Italy, Sybaris, as the terminal point on an overland route from the east to the west coast. Its foundation made it possible for goods to be shipped from Greece and Asia Minor to Sybaris itself on the east coast, transported westward overland to Poseidonia, thus avoiding the long sea journey around the tip of Italy and the dangerous passage through the straits of Messina, and from there sold to Etruscan or Italic customers. The scheme worked well enough to provide Poseidonia with a flourishing economy, strong enough to withstand the destruction of Sybaris, the mother city, by her rival Croton in 510 BC, and between the mid-6th and mid-5th centuries BC the three great Doric temples were built there which remain among the glories of Greek architecture. There is no reason to think that during this period relations were at all unfriendly between the Greeks and the native Italic population, both groups living side by side, but by the end of the 5th century BC the Italic successes further north prompted the Lucanians under either Samnite leadership or Samnite inspiration to attack Poseidonia and drive out the Greeks. From then until 273 BC, when it became a Roman colony, the city was in Samnite hands.

It is to this Samnite period that the painted tombs mentioned in Chapter

2 date, but before examining these 4th-century BC examples of Italic art we must look briefly at an earlier tomb, the Tomb of the Diver, which was painted around 470 BC. The fact that the paintings in the Tomb of the Diver were executed during Poseidonia's Greek days led the excavators, as we saw in Chapter 2, to claim them as Greek paintings. They certainly show the influence of Greek painted pottery, which was imported from Greece in large quantities and must have been familiar to the local artists responsible for the tomb decorations, but there is also evidence of strong Etruscan influence. Once again the Campanian artist is working with foreign ideas and even styles, but treating them in his own way. The scene which gives the tomb its name was painted on the inside of the lid, and shows the figure of a naked young man diving from a platform into a pool of blue-green water. There has been speculation as to whether the scene shows an actual sporting event or is in some way symbolic, representing a leap into the next world, so to speak. In the absence of any literary evidence on the subject it is probably safer to limit our observations to the style and content of the painting which, although it certainly shows an acquaintance with contemporary Greek methods of representing the human figure, finds its closest parallel in the Etruscan tombs of a generation earlier. In the Tarquinian Tomb of Hunting and Fishing, painted between 530 and 520 BC, there is a very similar figure of a diver, inserted into the same kind of naturalistic background. In both cases the composition shows nothing of the tightness of organization of Greek scenes of athletes, and the general air of realism – the sense of air and space, for example, and the interest in vegetation – reminds us not so much of archaic or Classical Greek art as of the Minoan frescoes of Bronze Age Greece: there is a surprising similarity between the diver from Paestum and the ivory statuette of an acrobat found at Knossos, and a number of frescoes from Knossos and other

Fragment of sculptural decoration from a building of the Samnite period at Pompeii. The motif, a gorgoneion, is Greek, but the treatment is Italic.

Minoan sites show the same interest in plant life. This does not mean, of course, that there is any direct connection between the Minoans and the artists of Poseidonia, separated as they are by 1,000 years; it does, however, illustrate how Italic artists, and Etruscan ones also, had returned to an interest in the natural world which was always present in Minoan art and which was never of major importance for the Greeks, preoccupied as they generally were with man as the center of existence.

The same kind of local variations on Greek and Etruscan themes can be seen on the paintings along the sides of the tomb. The scenes are of a kind familiar from Etruscan tombs, showing as they do banqueters and musicians taking part in the feast which formed part of the funeral ceremonies. The drawing of the figures, particularly in a scene in which a rosy-lipped boy is rejecting (without much conviction) the advances of an older, bearded man, shows a use of line which again brings to mind the style of contemporary Greek vase painting, but the anatomical inaccuracies, the massiveness of the figures, the general spirit of the paintings, all these are as close or closer to Etruscan models as to Greek. If the paintings in this tomb differ in quality and subject matter from others found at Paestum and elsewhere in southern Italy, it is probably because their artist was more aware of the work of his contemporaries elsewhere, both in Italy and abroad, and his interest is reflected in his work.

The other painted tombs discovered at Paestum, all of which date to the 4th century BC, are by comparison much more provincial. Their painters were obviously concerned to reproduce religious or ritual scenes that were important and meaningful to them, without worrying about the latest developments in artistic styles, and there is no attempt at accurate figural drawing or perspective. As so often in Italic art, however, lack of sophistication does not mean lack of effect, and the funeral processions and scenes of life beyond the grave often have a strange power of their own. In one example a procession of mourners makes its way along the lower part of the painting while the dead woman is shown in a scene above, being transported to the next life in a boat rowed by a winged female divinity, the representative of Death, who seems a combination of a Gorgon, the Greek ferryman Charon and the Etruscan deity Vanth. Many of the other figures of deities and monsters in these paintings seem close relatives of Etruscan ones, but the Samnites and other peoples of southern Italy do not seem to have shared the Etruscans' obsession with religion; although the evidence is scanty, the paintings do not show the almost morbid concern with ritual and consuming interest in interpreting the intentions of the gods for which the Etruscans were famous even in Roman times. Even in scenes of mourning or lamentation there is a sense of self-control and stolidity which is appropriate to a people of peasant stock. A frieze from a tomb at Ruvo, on the east coast of Italy, showing a procession of women performing a funeral dance, is all the more moving for its lack of overt emotion. And in the other tombs from Paestum scenes of gladiatorial combats, processions of warriors and depictions of weapons and armor serve as a reminder of the warlike character of the people for whom the tombs were painted: not even the Romans could accuse the Samnites of being lazy or pleasure-loving.

In general the Samnites and their Italic neighbors emerge as worthy enemies of the growing power of Rome. Not as politically conscious as the Etruscans, they were nevertheless capable of civic organization, as inscriptions from Pompeii show. During its Samnite period Pompeii was

Temple of Hera II, Paestum, c. 460 BC. Formerly called the Temple of Poseidon, this has now been identified as the later of two temples at Paestum which were dedicated to Hera.

governed by a series of local magistrates, the chief of whom bore the title of *meddix pumpaians*; others, perhaps borrowed from Roman models, included the *kvaisstor* and *aidilis*, equivalent to the Latin *quaestor* and *aedilis*. As this suggests, for much of the 4th century BC relations between Romans and Samnites were friendly enough. Both peoples had been threatened by a common enemy when the Gauls crossed the Alps at the end of the 5th century BC and in 390 BC sacked Rome. The Romans were under constant pressure from other Latin tribes and the Samnites had troubles of their own, in the form of a series of wars with the Greek city of Tarentum; and the result of all these dangers was a treaty of peace and friendship between the two peoples which was concluded in 354 BC. But possession of the *Ager Campanus*, the rich farmland of Campania, which had attracted in turn Greeks, Etruscans and Samnites, was too great a temptation for Rome to resist, and the following 60 years were marked by a series of bitter confrontations between the two which was only ended by the Samnites' final defeat in 290 BC. Our knowledge of the so-called Samnite Wars is derived mainly from the account provided by Livy, and is therefore strongly biased in favor of Rome, but he makes no attempt to hide the fact that the Samnites inflicted some crushing defeats upon the Roman forces. One of these, indeed, became almost legendary: in 321 BC an entire Roman army was tricked into invading central Campania and trapped in a mountain pass near Benevento known as the Caudine Forks, where it was forced to surrender and pass under the yoke. Centuries later the Roman poet Lucan, writing in the time of Nero, recalled the humiliation of this Samnite victory, which was mainly caused by the fact that the Roman troops, accustomed to fighting on level open ground, found it difficult to deal with opponents whose natural home was the mountains. But what the Samnites lacked was the ability to follow up their victories, or to be more fair, the drive for further territorial conquest which inspired the Romans: instead of taking the offensive they signed a defensive treaty which guaranteed the existing frontiers. Within a few years the Romans had once again taken the offensive, foiled the Samnites' attempt to form a grand anti-Roman coalition with Gauls, Umbrians and Etruscans, and by 290 BC finally crushed Samnite opposition. The chief Samnite cities were occupied and turned into Roman colonies; Poseidonia was colonized in 273 BC and its name changed to Paestum.

In the case of other peoples whom they had conquered the Romans were able, even after the most terrible struggles, to establish friendly relations; but this time both sides retained long and bitter memories of their encounters. For the Romans the Samnite Wars represented, as they saw it in retrospect, one of the most severe challenges to their mission to rule the world, a challenge no doubt all the more disturbing in that it came from a people who, unlike their subsequent Greek and Carthaginian enemies, had so much in common with them. The Samnites, for their part, 200 years later were to lead Italy's last attempt to win its independence from Rome when in 91 BC Italic tribes from central and southern Italy broke away and formed their own confederation. They established their capital at Corfinium in the Abruzzi and renamed it, with obvious symbolic intent, Italica. There they set up their own senate and magistracies and issued coinage with inscriptions in Latin and Oscan, bearing depictions of the Roman she-wolf being trampled by the Italic bull. But by a series of political concessions as much as military victories the Romans succeeded in splitting up the secessionists, and by 88 BC only the Samnites remained in

Tomb painting from Ruvo in Apulia, 5th–4th century BC. Museo Nazionale, Naples. Although influenced by contemporary Greek and Etruscan work, this procession of dancing mourners reflects the simplicity of its Italic origins.

implacable opposition to Roman domination. Not until 82 BC were they finally crushed, when a battle fought outside the very walls of Rome, by the Porta Collina, was won by Roman forces under Sulla, who characteristically followed up his victory by ordering the slaughter of all those Samnites who had been taken prisoner. The last representatives of Italic independence were thereby eliminated and Rome could continue its own painful transition from republic to empire.

The Apulians. If our knowledge of the Samnites is often incomplete and confused, it is nonetheless a model of clarity and precision in comparison with the picture we have of the native cultures of Apulia and Calabria. To a great extent our Roman sources are to blame for much of this, with their apparently casual interchange of one name for another in their written references to the pre-Roman inhabitants of the deep south. In Calabria, for example, ancient writers refer to Italians, Ausonians, Opicians, Oenotrians and others without ever making clear to what extent the various names represent separate peoples or are simply alternatives for a single race. It is perhaps unfair, though, to expect from them any real coherence in dealing with what must have been even in Roman times a mass of legend, tradition and barely surviving memories. On the whole the only safe conclusion to draw from the literary evidence is that the Romans applied these and other terms comparatively indiscriminately to those peoples who had preceded them in Italy and whose culture was recognizably distinct from that of Greek and other foreign immigrants. In the opening book of the *Aeneid*, for example, Aeneas' lieutenant Ilioneus obviously feels somewhat embarrassed by the imprecision of his knowledge in explaining to the

Top: Daunian vase with geometric designs and elaborate three-dimensional decoration, 6th century BC. The fantastic shape and abstract patterns represent a deliberate rejection of contemporary Greek styles. Museo Archeologico, Bari.

Above: Double-spouted flask, late 5th–early 4th century BC. Although it is in the same tradition as earlier examples of Daunian pottery, the more restrained decoration and the use of motifs like the spiral indicate a growing Greek influence. Museo Archeologico, Bari.

Carthaginian queen Dido where the Trojan exiles are bound for: "There is a land called by the Greeks the country of the west, ancient, powerful and prosperous: the Oenotrians settled it, and their descendants, or so we hear, now call it Italy after the name of its founder." The term "Oenotrians" is often used by ancient writers for various early inhabitants of Italy, but without any great consistency. In commenting on this very passage the 4th-century AD grammarian Servius provides us with a perfect illustration of the ancient world's undiscriminating approach to problems of archaeology or anthropology, in an explanation that is a masterpiece of improbability and scholarly confusion: "The name Oenotria is either derived from the words *vino optimo* (excellent wine), which is produced in Italy, or from Oenotrus, king of the Sabines, or, according to some from Oenotrus, the brother of Italus, who came to Italy from Greece with the Pelasgians." With help like this it is hardly surprising that modern archaeologists have had a hard time in relating their discoveries to the historical tradition, particularly since the superimposed Greek culture is particularly rich in Calabria and therefore serves to provide further confusion.

Nonetheless in Apulia, at least, a picture is beginning to emerge. The north, around the modern city of Foggia, was the territory of the Dauni; in central Apulia, around modern Bari, were the Peucetii, and in the south the Messapii. The latter were sometimes called by the ancients the Iapyges, although this name was also often used for all the inhabitants of Apulia – all three of the above groups, that is – who were in addition sometimes called Salentini or simply Apuli. At any rate all these peoples, whatever their names, shared a basically similar culture and language which show connections with those of the Italic peoples to the west, but also individual peculiarities. Clearly the geographical position of Apulia, which is the part of Italy most accessible from the east, had a major impact on its development, and already in the Bronze Age the Mycenaeans had arrived there and established a trading post near the site of the future city of Tarentum. Throughout the early part of the Iron Age Apulia retained its contacts with Greece and the eastern Adriatic, and at the end of the 8th century BC Tarentum was founded by Greek settlers from Sparta. Their reason for leaving their homeland was a curious one, incidentally, and one that throws some light on the motives of the early Greek colonizers. Far from wanting to spread abroad the glories of a culture which they believed superior, in the manner of a Cecil Rhodes, the future Tarentines were a group of illegitimate children who had been conceived and born in Sparta during a time of war, when the Spartan army was away from home and only a few young men had been left behind or sent back. As the children grew up they began to resent their subordinate status and, in order to prevent trouble, were persuaded to leave home and settle elsewhere.

It would seem, therefore, as if Apulia would be of all parts of Italy the most exposed to Greek influence and the most likely to be fully Hellenized; but paradoxically this was not what happened. The continuity of culture there throughout the Late Bronze and Early Iron Ages had created a people who had sufficient cultural independence to survive the impact of foreign ideas, and in fact retain that independence down to Roman times. While in Sicily the decline at the end of the Bronze Age had left the native peoples weakened and in a condition favorable to the wholesale adoption of a new way of life when the Greeks arrived, the Apulians, on the other hand, were able to continue to draw on Greek ideas while remaining recognizably distinct. It is not clear to what extent this produced actual conflict between

Greeks and Apulians, but it is significant that Taranto was to be the only Greek colony founded there. Furthermore, in some cases at least, the new Greek arrivals, far from imposing their own culture, were absorbed by the people already established there. A vase from Bari, painted in the local manner, has a running animal on it above which is written a Greek word; it is presumably the work of a Greek artist who is completely under the influence of the native style.

This native style, so strikingly devoid of Greek influence, first appeared at the end of the 9th century BC and seems mainly derived from pottery of the Late Bronze Age in Italy. The vessels are large with wide bodies, and brightly painted; their most characteristic shape is the so-called *trozzella*, which in the dialect of modern Puglia means little wheel; it consists of a round belly with tall narrow handles decorated with small disks which look like wheels. Their most striking feature, however, and one that contrasts most strongly with contemporary Greek pottery, is the use of three-dimensional decorations which are added to the handle or elsewhere; sometimes abstract, sometimes naturalistic, these elaborate additions often strike a grotesque note which seems to relate the Apulians to Italic cultures elsewhere in Early Iron Age Italy. The painted decorations are for the most part rigidly geometric, and although there are some local variations between Daunian, Peucetian and Messapian styles, all of them retain the same distinctiveness. Nor were these pots produced only for local consumption: they were exported not only to other peoples in Italy, the Picenes for example, but even across the Adriatic to the west coast of Illyria, suggesting that their makers may have learned something from the Greeks' business acumen.

Meanwhile, in the last few years, large numbers of engraved and painted stone slabs have been found which further enrich our knowledge of Apulian culture. Most of them came from the Daunian centers of northern Apulia, in particular the city of Siponto. Like the Ligurian stelae we saw in Chapter 3 they take the form of schematized representations of human figures often equipped with jewelry and weapons, but the detail is much more elaborate than in the Ligurian examples. The dresses of the standing figures are decorated with complex designs, often geometric but also sometimes showing human and animal forms. These stones were apparently originally used as grave markers, although unfortunately they have never been found in their original positions, having been removed at a later period and used as building material; the scenes of processions and hunts that some of them show have a narrative quality that seems reminiscent of the situla art of the Este people, a reminder that the Apulians, the Picenes and the Este people must have been subject to considerable common influence and interchange as a result of their position on the east coast, cut off both geographically and psychologically from the rest of Italy by the Apennines. For the moment our knowledge of the Apulians is mainly limited to their vases and stone grave markers, but recent years have seen an increasing number of finds of other types. Excavation of Messapian tombs has produced paintings and bronze fibulae, and archaeologists have begun to uncover the remains of Apulian settlements. At Gravina a Peucetian settlement has been discovered, as well as tombs containing Greek vases, and two important Messapian towns are still in the process of being excavated. At the first of these, Ugento and its nearby port, in addition to tombs, a shrine to Artemis from the 6th century BC and fortifications and homes from later periods, there came to light a

Stone stele from Siponto in northern Apulia, 7th century BC. Manfredonia Museum. The carved human figure is almost hidden by the profusion of decorative detail: some of the geometric designs are similar to those on contemporary pottery.

Right: South Italian vases are frequently decorated, as here, with scenes from Greek mythology, but the style is much more exuberant than that of their Attic counterparts. The subject in this case is the death of Cassandra at the hands of Ajax, with Apollo looking on. British Museum, London.

Opposite: Bell krater from Paestum painted by Asteas, mid-4th century BC. Vatican Museums. It shows a scene from a *phlyax* play involving Zeus and Hermes, both of them portrayed with comic grotesqueness.

splendid bronze statue of Poseidon, clearly of Greek workmanship. The other site, Cavallino, was first occupied in the Bronze Age, and a later town there was inhabited from the 8th to the 6th century BC, when Greek influence had begun to increase. These and other sites are gradually revealing more and more information about their inhabitants' origins, cultures and relations with the Greeks, and although much still remains confused, there is at least hope that one day our knowledge of a people who are among the most fascinating of early Italians will be more satisfactory.

Foreigners in Italy. Although the Greeks were by far the most influential foreigners in Italy, they were not the only ones. Towards the end of the 8th century BC, at around the same time that eastern Sicily was being colonized by Greek settlers, Phoenicians were arriving in the western part of the island; indeed Thucydides believed that the Phoenicians were already established in Sicily when the Greeks arrived and were driven west by them, although this is not supported by any archaeological evidence. It seems far more likely that the attention of the Phoenicians was first attracted to Sicily by the presence of their Greek trade competitors, and that they saw a Phoenician presence there as a way to limit Greek expansion in Sicily while developing a trade route westward that led from western Sicily via the Phoenician colony of Carthage in North Africa to southern Spain with its silver and other mineral resources. The following century saw a number of Phoenician colonies established on or near the west coast of the island, including Motya and Panormus – the latter to become Palermo, the largest city of modern Sicily. The Greeks and Etruscans between them seem to have prevented the Phoenicians from establishing independent colonies on the Italian mainland, although they were able to

EUROPEO

Restoring the Riace Bronzes

The completion of an archeological odyssey

— GIAN LUIGI GONANO —

Gian Luigi Gonano writes for the newsmagazine "Europeo" of Milan, from which this is excerpted.

Now that the "bronzes of Riace" are ready to leave Florence on their way back to the National Museum of Reggio Calabria, the long, difficult odyssey of their restoration can finally be considered. After the 2,500-year-old Greek statues were discovered by a Roman archeology buff in August, 1972, on the ocean bottom near Riace Marina, the museum at Reggio Calabria undertook a preliminary scaling of the rock-hard crust that covered them. Two and a half years of this work made it clear that the

cleaned by immersion in stabilizing baths that will prolong their resistance to corrosion. Technician Ulisse Lazzeri explains the process: "We prepared special hoists, and extra-large tubs into which the statues were repeatedly immersed in an ammonia-alcohol solution. Then a year of observation followed, during which we kept the bronzes in what we call 'the room of death,' where the humidity is at a very high level so we can gauge the reappearance of corrosion. Where it occurred we treated the statues with a benzoin solution and Paraloid B72, which forms an extremely thin protective skin."

In 1980 the job was finished, and the center, which had documented the entire operation through photographs and graphs for the use of scholars, decided to publicize its work and the men behind it with an exhibition titled "The Great Bronzes of Riace — An Archeological Restoration." It was supposed to last just over a month, but the crowds grew as the merely curious mingled with art and history scholars. Six months and several hundred thousand visitors later, the statues, after a stopover in Rome, are at last ready to be returned to Reggio Calabria.

■

(June 29)

um's resources were insufficient for the job, and the statues were transferred to the Center for Restoration at the Tuscan Archeological Bureau in Florence.

Restoration of the statues began with a graphic, photographic, and radiographic documentation of their state. When X-ray equipment at the center proved inadequate for the job, the statues were taken to a major surgical firm, where ultra-powerful gamma rays disclosed the thickness of the metal; the areas of the joints, solderings, and wedges; and the consistency of the interior. When they returned to the center the bronzes underwent a microscopic analysis that determined their crystallography, impurities, and heat levels—and thus the technology employed in making them.

An electric-arc spectrograph ionized a sample of the material and photographed its spectrum. This was compared with the spectrum of the same elements in their pure state, allowing researchers to separate principal elements from trace materials and thus identify the geological deposits from which the original raw materials were mined.

After these examinations, the hard crust was removed from the statues with brushes,

Riace statue—"crowds grew." JB/Keystone

scalpels, turbine-driven pneumatic hammers, and ultrasonic apparatus. The interior was a different matter. The marine environment, free of temperature leaps and oxygen, with a constant humidity, had favored preservation, but the atmosphere out of water set loose a process of corrosion that would ultimately have destroyed the bronzes.

Roberto Del Francia, director of the restoration center, tells the story of this phase: "We removed the lead studs in the feet that originally fixed the statues to their bases, and through those openings we forced oxygenated water to soften the encrustations. Then we proceeded with steel shafts armed with scrapers, hooks, and scoops; at times we even had to improvise the tools we needed. This work lasted one year."

In the final step the bronzes were

Temple of Concord, Agrigento, c. 440 BC. The temple, made of local stone, is roughly contemporary with the Parthenon. Its fine state of preservation is due to the fact that it was converted into a church.

plant settlements on the coasts of both Sardinia and Corsica, and there may well have been Phoenician traders living as foreigners in a number of Etruscan and Greek cities. As we saw in the last chapter, recent finds at Etruscan Pyrgi have included a temple to the Phoenician goddess Astarte, as well as the famous inscriptions in Etruscan and Phoenician. In addition, some scholars believe that there was even a Phoenician community in 7th-century BC Rome, trading there and worshiping their god Melqart in the Forum Boarium. Whatever the degree of actual Phoenician presence on Italian soil though, there can be no doubt that Phoenician ships played a large part in the complex trading patterns that linked Greeks, Etruscans and Carthaginians, and the various alliances that were concluded between the three major powers of the western Mediterranean conditioned much of the history of Italy in the 6th and 5th centuries BC. In general these alliances were characterized by mutual dislike and mistrust, and dictated only by temporary expedience. Our knowledge of Phoenician literature is too scanty to give us any idea of their feelings about Greeks or Etruscans, but as early as the composition of the *Odyssey* the Greeks made their own opinions about the Phoenicians perfectly clear, when Odysseus describes a Phoenician merchant as "a man who knew all the tricks, always swallowing up what he could, a real trouble maker." No doubt the feelings were mutual. Ironically enough it was the Romans who benefited most in the end, for after a combined Etruscan and Carthaginian fleet had defeated the Greek colonists from Phocaea in 540 BC, the Etruscan navy suffered disastrous losses in 474 BC at Cumae, leaving only the Carthaginians to face the Romans in the Punic Wars – unsuccessfully, of course.

But if the influence of the Phoenicians in Italy was mainly economic and military, that of the Greeks was all-pervading. From their first arrival in the 8th century BC their impact on Sicily, the Etruscans, the Italic peoples and Rome itself was immense and lasting. The first Greek colonists to land in Ischia began a tradition of Hellenization and Philhellenism in Italy that led the Roman satirist Juvenal to exclaim of Rome, as late as the 2nd century AD: "I can not bear this city gone Greek . . . these Greeks think so quickly, they are utterly without scruples, quick talkers . . . what do you think that fellow over there is? he can be anything you want – an expert on grammar, rhetoric, geometry, a painter, wrestling coach, soothsayer, tightrope walker, doctor, magician: these hungry little Greeks know everything. Tell one to go to heaven and he'll fly up there." The rhetoric of xenophobia is clearly recognizable; unappealing as it may be, however, it reveals how neither the collapse of the Greek cities in Italy and Sicily in the 4th and 3rd centuries BC nor the conquest of mainland Greece, first by Alexander the Great and finally by Rome, prevented the spread of Greek culture. This is not the place for a detailed analysis of that culture or its effect on the Romans, but no picture of early Italy would be complete without a brief glance at the Greek settlers there.

As we saw in the case of the Spartans who founded Tarentum, the Greeks who moved westwards to find new homes were motivated often by necessity rather than idealism. Overpopulation or unfavorable political conditions at home, the search for new markets or fresh supplies of raw materials, seem to have been the most common reasons for emigration. Under pressures of this kind many Greeks moved east to Asia Minor or south to Egypt, but Italy and Sicily also offered attractive possibilities to the first colonists and the cities they founded there became the richest in the entire Greek world. Their temples and other buildings were of vast size and their art so elaborate as to seem at times ostentatious. The prosperity that successful trading won them gained them also the reputation of being big luxury lovers and spendthrifts: the name of one of their greatest cities, Sybaris, has after all entered our language with a not altogether favorable significance. This new greater Greece founded in the west, Magna Graecia, has sometimes been compared with that other New World colonized by settlers moving westwards, where everything is bigger, better, richer and more extravagant than in the mother country. Certainly the mixture of admiration and envy with which mainland Greece looked to Greek Italy has its modern parallels, as does the way in which Magna Graecia increasingly attracted some of the leading cultural figures of the old country. Aeschylus twice visited Sicily and died there in 456 BC; he even wrote a play (now lost) called *The Women of Etna* in honor of the Syracusan king Hieron I, the same Hieron who had helped the Cumaeans to defeat the Etruscans in 474 BC, and the picture of Aeschylus walking on the beach at Gela only a few years before the Samnite occupation of Pompeii is an intriguing one. A little later Herodotus was among the Athenians who took part in the founding of the colony of Thurii near the site of Sybaris on the gulf of Taranto, where he died in 420 BC; and in the following century Plato made a number of visits to Italy and Sicily. After an initial journey to the west he was invited back to Syracuse in 368 BC, as "visiting expert" so to speak, to put his theories into practice and turn the new ruler of Syracuse, Dionysius II, into a "philosopher-king"; his total lack of success did not deter him from making a further, equally unsuccessful attempt in 362 BC, and he retained an interest in Sicilian politics until the murder of his patron Dion in 354 BC.

But although distinguished visitors were always welcome, Sicilian and south Italian Greek art often went its own way. In the field of painted pottery, for example, by the end of the 5th century BC the Greek cities had begun to make and paint their own vases instead of importing them from

Top: Head of a girl, perhaps Artemis or Aphrodite, late 4th or early 3rd century BC. Museo Archeologico, Taranto. The piece is of Parian marble, and stylistically very similar to the work of Praxiteles, although some scholars believe it to be a Roman copy of a lost Greek work.

Above: Terracotta head of a goddess from Medma on the west coast of Calabria (a colony founded by Locri), early 5th century BC. Museo Nazionale, Reggio di Calabria. Height c. 25 cm. The head may represent Athene and perhaps comes from a group which decorated a temple.

Decorated bronze mirror, early 5th century BC.
Museo Nazionale, Reggio di Calabria.

Athens. Local schools were quick to develop, first in the east in Lucania and around Tarentum, and then in Sicily. Political events certainly affected this sudden upsurge of local manufacture: the Peloponnesian War made trade difficult if not impossible, and the Athenians' attack on Syracuse, ending in their defeat in 413 BC, meant that if the Sicilians wanted painted pottery they would have to make their own. By the beginning of the 4th century BC Sicilian artists had spread to Campania, where they set up their workshops and developed another series of styles.

These south Italian vases, over 10,000 of which have been found, are far less austere than their Attic counterparts. Their painters show an almost baroque taste for elaborate, extravagant ornamentation, bold use of perspective and massive size. Their subject matter, too, is often broad in theme: scenes from tragedies are common, as well as episodes from *phlyax* plays, a kind of farce which often parodied heroic themes, which are especially useful for evidence on Greek theatrical practices, in addition to providing a more relaxed picture of south Italian taste. Other vases show funerary or wedding scenes. South Italian pottery rarely achieves the technical finish and perfection of vases imported from Greece, but it often conveys something of the spirit of adventure of its painters.

Sculptors and architects, too, were attracted by the possibilities of large commissions for creating exciting new works. The Greek temple took on fresh aspects when it stood in a different landscape, and the temples at Poseidonia and elsewhere show a power and imagination of design and construction which may be equaled but not surpassed in Greece itself. In Sicily the problem of designing temples not for natural settings as at Sunium or Bassae but for the urban environment of great cities like Akragas (modern Agrigento) produced startling solutions. The Temple of Olympian Zeus there, which was probably begun at the end of the 6th century BC, is staggering both in its size and in the novelty of its design. The base was over 170 feet by over 360 feet, the facade was decorated with a series of Doric half-columns some 13 feet in diameter, and incorporated into the building were a series of colossal giant statues, or *telamones*, each one over 25 feet tall. Akragas was sacked by the Carthaginians in 405 BC, before the temple was finished, and work was never resumed, so that our knowledge of it remains incomplete. Subsequent events served to increase the damage further: in 1401 AD an earthquake brought down those columns which were still standing, and in the 18th century many of the stones were used to construct the jetties at the nearby harbor of Porto Empedocle. Even today, however, the ruins of this monumental building are impressive enough, and if it had been completed it would have stood as a fitting symbol of the wealth, intellectual daring and artistic ambition of Greek Sicily.

But the fact that the temple was not completed is itself symbolic. The successes of cities like Tarentum, Syracuse, Locri and others were achieved in a world that was far from peaceful. We have already seen the effects of the continual tensions between Greeks, Carthaginians, Etruscans and others; added to those was the permanent inability of the Greeks themselves to establish peaceful relations with one another. Old quarrels between mother cities at home were brought to Italy by the colonists and refought there, or new causes for grievances were developed locally. The suicidal inability of the Greeks to unite – except at times of the most terrible external threat, as at the time of the Persian Wars – had its effect also in the west. No city was wealthier than Sybaris, founded at the end of the 8th

century BC, with its rich farmland, its famous wine and its legendary extravagance, but in 510 BC Sybaris was completely destroyed by her Greek neighbor and rival Croton. Not satisfied with the defeat of Sybaris, Croton decided to obliterate all trace of the conquered city by diverting a local river, the Crathis, and burying it beneath tons of mud and silt: only in the last few years have archaeologists begun to undo the damage so mercilessly and deliberately caused, and initiated explorations in the area of the buried city, in a project that became known as the "Search for Sybaris." Between 1960 and 1965 a series of joint campaigns conducted by the Pennsylvania University Museum and the Lerici Foundation (whom we met in Chapter 2 looking for Etruscan tombs) used electronic probes to locate submerged features, and then drained certain selected areas for detailed excavation: among the buildings uncovered has been a theater. Since 1969 in further campaigns Italian archaeologists have explored other areas, including what may be a shipyard, but the work is slow and difficult and moreover extremely expensive. It is a curious historical irony that the exploration of an ancient city so famous for its wealth should be hampered by modern-day lack of funds. But there is some comfort in the fact that, just as in the case of other peoples elsewhere in Italy, the Greek cities will be providing us with exciting new discoveries for a long time to come.

Terracotta plaque from Locri, 470–460 BC. Museo Nazionale, Reggio di Calabria. Height *c.* 27 cm. This is one of a series of votive tablets found in storage pits at Locri early this century: they are connected with the mystery cult of Demeter and Kore, and seem to show scenes from the life of Kore.

Funerary Art at Paestum

I

With the exception of the Tomb of the Diver, of c. 470 BC, the painted tombs of Paestum all date to the last half of the 4th century BC, when the city was under Italic domination. Frequently unsophisticated and even crude in style, they nonetheless provide a precious insight into the world of their creators, not so much in terms of information about daily life as about the Italic attitude to death. It must be admitted that the general picture is not a comforting one. Scenes of lamentation alternate with violent and bloody confrontations between man and man, and beast and beast, and the general mood is somber and gloomy. Yet the very simplicity of style produces an impressive dignity and self-control.

1 In this scene of boxing, from the funeral games, the gulf between these paintings and contemporary Greek art becomes apparent. Some attempt is made to render the anatomy of the two figures, but the foreshortening is not always successful and there is little sense of movement.

2 In the upper register the dead woman is seen climbing into the boat which will carry her to the underworld. Its ferryman, the local version of the Greek Charon and the Etruscan Charun, turns towards us with his ferocious smile, inherited from the Gorgon heads of earlier Greek and Etruscan art. Below, a scene of propitiatory sacrifice and offerings.

3 Prothesis, or lying in state, second half of the 4th century BC. The dead woman lies on her bier, while two companions perform the time-honored Mediterranean gestures of grief and lamentation, tearing the hair and beating the breasts.

4 Two Samnite foot soldiers, one of them carrying a standard. The elaborate helmets suggest that the scene represented is a ceremonial procession rather than an actual combat. This painting comes from an earlier find, and is now in the Museo Archeologico, Naples.

5 Horseman accompanying funeral procession or possibly the dead man journeying to the next world. His downcast head and right hand leaning back create a mood of weariness which perhaps supports the latter identification.

2

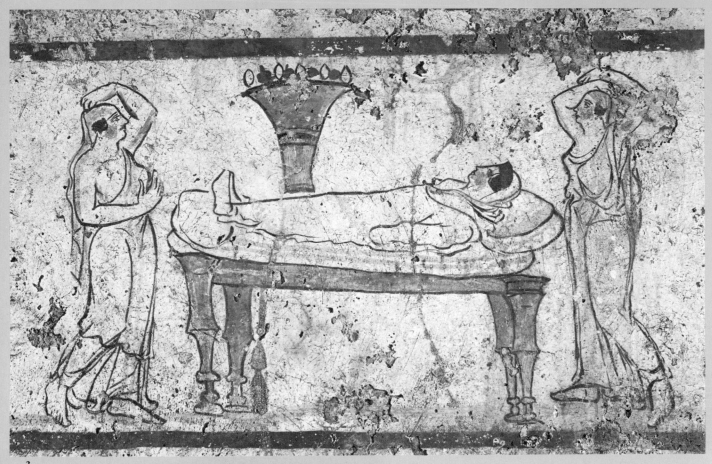

3

4

5

6 Diagram of the disposition of the painted slabs which make up the Tomb of the Diver. The four vertical slabs which form the walls of the tomb are almost completely buried underground, and the scene showing the diver is painted on the inside of the lid. After Pallottino.

7 Banqueting scene from the Tomb of the Diver. To the right a young man makes a token attempt to resist the amorous advances of his older companion, while on the far left another young man stares rather thoughtfully ahead. The banqueters in the center seem to be playing *kottabos*, a game invented in Sicily and borrowed by the Greeks which seems to have consisted of tossing drops of wine on to a predetermined target, although one of the players seems rather more interested in the scene to his left.

8 An episode from the Tomb of the Diver. The figure dressed in white may be a new arrival at the banquet in progress on the other wall, although some commentators have suggested that he represents the dead man being escorted to the underworld.

9 Chariot race, part of the funeral games. The custom of including events such as this in the funeral rituals had been followed since Homeric times. The style here is not very careful, but immensely vivid.

10 Scene of hunting. The dogs biting the stag seem to be borrowed from Greek depictions of the death of Actaeon. Although little attempt is made to render perspective, the episode is lively and full of movement.

11 Two griffins attack a panther. The violent assault of mythological beasts on a creature of the real world finds a parallel in the frescoes of the François tomb at Vulci. If it is not intended to convey something of the disquiet with which its painter contemplated the next life, its purpose may be apotropaic (to keep away evil spirits).

6

8

7

9

10

11

6 THE ROMAN LEGACY

The impact of Rome upon the development of our civilization has been immense and far reaching. In language, laws, politics, art, religion and many other ways the Roman legacy continues to condition our daily lives: much of western Europe, for instance, still uses a road network based on that devised and constructed by the Romans. Part of this impact is due to the inventive and industrious nature of the Roman character itself, but at the same time as the spread of Roman power produced the diffusions of Roman culture, it also permitted the spread of the ideas of the other peoples on which Roman culture had drawn. It was through Rome, for example, that Greek artistic and literary styles attained their widest circulation and passed into western tradition, and the rapid spread of Christianity dates from the time when it was adopted as the official religion of the Roman Empire.

These represent perhaps the two most significant cases of Rome's transmission to us of ideas which were not their own, but in other ways too the Roman legacy includes elements which the Romans themselves, sometimes unconsciously, had inherited from others. The part played by the native peoples of Italy in the development of Roman culture is certainly less obvious and less spectacular than that played by the Greeks, but almost all the peoples we have seen in this book made their contribution, often involuntarily, to the growth of Rome and its culture and thereby helped to form our own world. We have already seen the Romans at a later stage in their development in contact with Samnites, Etruscans and others, but the influences are deeper rooted, and in order to assess the effects of these peoples upon the Romans we must go back to the earliest stages of Roman culture and the foundation of the city.

The foundation of Rome. The late 8th century BC was a period of great activity in Italy. The Greeks had arrived in the south and in Sicily. In central Italy Villanovan culture was being increasingly supplanted by the Etruscans, although further north the great Villanovan center of Bologna was still at the height of its prosperity. To the east the Este people and the Apulians had already begun to develop their own distinctive cultural styles, while on Sardinia the native population was rebuilding old *nuraghi* and constructing new ones, probably in response to the growing presence of the Phoenicians in the western Mediterranean. Meanwhile in Latium and the mountains to the east of it, the Latin and Italic tribes were establishing their own individual village settlements. It says something for the unpredictability of history and human behavior that from all this cultural ferment there should have emerged one small Latin village which over the succeeding centuries would gain control not only over Italy and its peoples, but the greater part of the known world, and in the process would leave its

Lararium, or shrine to the Lares, the household gods, two of whom are shown holding a cornucopia as a symbol of abundance. This example comes from the House of Vettii at Pompeii.

mark on the future development of western civilization. The growth of Rome seemed to its later inhabitants inevitable, a proof of the favor of the gods and the unique character of her citizens. Even if with the benefit of hindsight we can add to those factors the additional ones of chance, good luck, and the errors and miscalculations of their opponents, in particular their fatal inability ever to unite against a common enemy, the Roman achievement remains immensely impressive. Modern archaeological discoveries have made it even more impressive by uncovering the humble origins and erratic first developments of this future ruler of the world: the Romans' own grandiose idea of the early regal days of their city has been replaced by a much more modest picture of early Rome, which only seems to emphasize its subsequent rise to power.

In the field of the early history of Rome, however, as in so many other areas touched on in this book, scholarly controversy is heated, and the increasing quantity of archaeological material produced by recent excavations has been subjected to a variety of interpretations. The continual difficulty has been to relate the archaeological finds to the literary

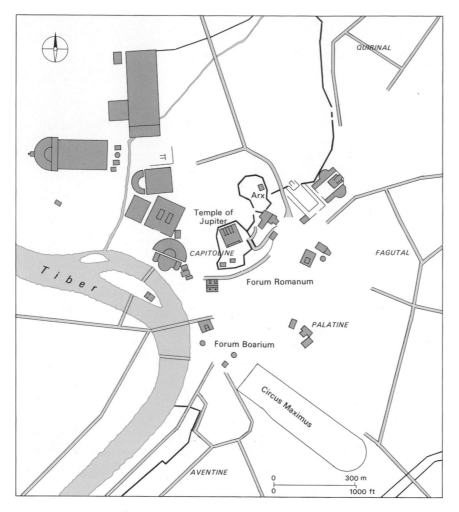

tradition handed down to us by the Romans themselves. If for the Apulians or even the Etruscans we must rely only on archaeological evidence with no written history to help, in the case of early Rome there is an embarrassment of riches in the detailed accounts provided by later Roman historians of events which occurred for the most part some 500 years before their time. Unfortunately the very precision of their accounts often makes them suspect: the accuracy of their sources – if and when they used any – is doubtful, and parallels between events in Roman history and in Greek are suspicious. (It is striking, for example, that according to Livy's account of the Roman conquest of Veii the siege there lasted exactly as long as the Greeks' siege of Troy.) All the literary evidence needs to be very carefully sifted and evaluated, therefore, but that does not mean, of course, that in contrast the archaeological evidence or its interpretation is always crystal-clear. Much of the material has been made available in a series of six volumes under the general title of *Early Rome,* by the great Swedish archaeologist Einar Gjerstad, but by no means all of his conclusions have been universally accepted. A particularly thorny problem, for example, has been the dating of the first growth of an individual community at the site of the future city, which Gjerstad placed at around 800 BC. A more controversial opinion is that of H. Müller-Karpe who believes that Rome's beginnings go back as far as the 10th century BC, and were subject to influence from the eastern Mediterranean. In general it is probably fair to say that, although we know a great deal more about the earliest history of their city and the Etruscan period which followed than the Romans themselves did, and the general sequence of events is becoming increasingly clear, much of the chronology remains still uncertain. It is certainly if regrettably true that simplified accounts of the period, such as the one which follows, are in danger of concealing many of the difficulties that remain and proving dangerously misleading: the reader is warned.

Recent finds of Apennine-style pottery have shown that a small community probably already existed on or near the Capitoline hill in the Middle Bronze Age, and Rome may even have been inhabited at the end of the Neolithic period, but there is no real evidence of a continuity of occupation, and the first settlements of the Early Iron Age seem to indicate a new beginning. Like other groups of Latins elsewhere in Latium, the first Romans were probably farmers and shepherds, and the simple groups of huts which were established on the hills which were to become so famous in later days, the Palatine, the Esquiline and others, are not substantially different from those of other tribes to their immediate south and east. In some respects, it is true, the Roman settlements themselves show certain internal variations: the villagers on the Palatine cremated their dead while the others preferred inhumation, and there is some variety of pottery styles. But although this seems to suggest that the first settlers were drawn from two or more separate groups of Latins, those groups were closely related in origins and culture, both to one another and to their neighbors.

Why did these early farmers choose Rome as the place to build their huts? Later Roman writers were ready with an answer: "Gods and men had good reasons for choosing this as the place to found a city: healthy hill-country, a river which was convenient for bringing supplies from inland and importing goods by sea, a spot near enough to the sea to make trade possible but not too close to be exposed to attack by foreign fleets, in the very center of Italy. The site was uniquely equipped to encourage the growth of the city." Livy's optimistic picture of the healthy climate of Rome will probably not be shared by those who have lived through the enervating heat of a Roman summer; nor was it shared by many of his Augustan contemporaries, the richer of whom left the city when they could for their villas in the hills or as far south as the Bay of Naples. Furthermore the convenience of the Tiber is severely limited by the fact that its mouth has always been liable to silt up and thereby prevent access to the sea, while further inland it is far from easy to navigate. Nor did Rome's geographical position ever provide it with a convenient harbor: later Roman emperors were driven to spend considerable time, energy and money on the construction of artificial port facilities, and even today, although Rome is only some 30 miles from the coast, sea passengers generally arrive at Naples or Genoa. The Bay of Naples would, in fact, have been an ideal location in many ways for the growth of a great Mediterranean power, with many advantages not shared by the site of Rome, as Greeks, Etruscans and Samnites were all to realize. By overestimating the wisdom of their remote ancestors, the Romans of Livy's day underestimated their own achievements.

The site of Rome was in fact more suitable to a pastoral community than a future imperial power. The earliest settlers constructed their huts on the summits of the hills around the valley of the Tiber, leaving the land around available for grazing. As the villages grew, the slopes of the hills, which in the early days were used only for tombs, became inhabited also, and by the end of the 7th century BC the large open space at the foot of the Capitoline and Palatine hills, later to become the Forum Romanum, had been partially

Above: The Forum Romanum, with the three surviving columns of the Temple of Castor and Pollux on the right and the small Temple of Vesta, partially reconstructed, on the left.

Above left: Plan of the city of Rome in the Republican period.

Left: Foundations of the round huts of the early settlers on the Palatine, dating to around 900 BC and the transition from the Bronze Age to the Early Iron Age. They suggest a simple pastoral community, perhaps grazing their flocks on the slopes of the Palatine and burying their dead around the marshy valley below, the site of the future Forum. The earliest tombs, however, were probably on the Palatine itself, where a very early example has been excavated.

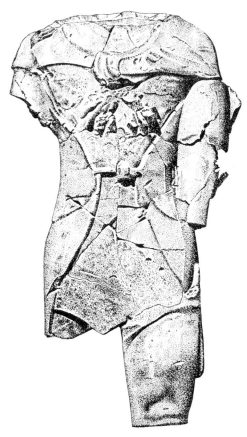

Terracotta statue of Herakles (recognizable from the lionskin knotted across his chest), dating to the late 6th century. It decorated a sanctuary near the church of Sant'Omobono, where earlier shrines had been constructed in the 7th and early 6th centuries. The building from which the statue of Herakles comes was itself destroyed a few years after it was built, perhaps at the time of the expulsion of the Etruscan kings around 510 BC.

drained and settled. Throughout this last period the simple village communities began for the first time to establish some contact with the outside world and import pottery and metalwork from the nearby Etruscan cities of Veii and Cerveteri.

Up to the arrival of the Etruscans, then, Rome remained just one of a number of Latin and Italic villages, growing more rapidly perhaps, but still culturally attached to a Latin tradition. We can see the results of this in religious terms in the worship of the god Mars, who was not only the divine father of the traditional founder of the city, Romulus, but who throughout Roman history occupied a central position in many of the most sacred of Roman rituals. Although a later emphasis on one of his aspects and his association with the Greek god Ares mean that Mars came to be generally considered the god of war, he was originally equally associated with fertility and farming. As the god of fertility his name was given to the first month of spring, our March, which was also the first month of the Roman year. In the annual ceremony of the *ambarvalia*, in which the fields were blessed, it was Mars whose help was invoked, and one of the earliest of all Latin hymns calls upon him. This is the famous hymn of the Arval Brothers, a religious association which was said to have been founded by Romulus himself, some of the records of which were preserved on marble tablets later discovered on the site of their meeting place just outside Rome. The inscriptions date from a much later period (14–241 AD), but they include a ritual hymn which must go back in its original form to the earliest period of Roman history. The meaning of the invocation is far from certain, but it seems to say: "Help us, o Lares, and you, Mars, do not let there be more destruction; be satisfied, fierce Mars, leap on to the threshold and stay there; call in turn upon all the spirits of sowing; help us, o Mars; dance!" In this emphasis on the twin aspects of Mars as god of both war and fertility, the early Romans were following the religious traditions of their Latin and Italic brothers; the Eugubian tables show that Mars was also an important deity for the Umbrians, while the Sabines and Oscans worshiped him under the name Mamers. At a later time, as their horizons expanded, the Romans preferred to think of themselves as related to the mainstream of east Mediterranean tradition, rather than the local Italic one, and their religion developed accordingly. But although in the process they devised a new account of their origins, which connected the foundation of Rome to the story of the fall of Troy and the wanderings of Aeneas, the association of its earliest days with the kind of rustic ceremony recalled by the hymn of the Arval Brothers remained profound. As late as the 5th century AD Rome's actual birthday was celebrated annually on 21 April, the day of the festival of the Palilia, in which shepherds and herdsmen purified their land and flocks for the coming year, using the blood of a horse that had been sacrificed to Mars the previous October, and the entire population of Rome and the countryside around concluded the day with an open-air feast. As we shall see, many of these early beliefs survived the introduction of more sophisticated ideas by the Etruscans and others.

Etruscan Rome. Although Rome was soon to fall under the political and cultural domination of the Etruscans, it is important to realize the Italic nature of her origins, since it played an important if sometimes secondary part in her development; nonetheless the arrival of the Etruscans marked the first major leap forward in the development of the city. The dates of the Etruscan period are in some doubt: our Roman sources state with characteristic precision that the period of Etruscan domination lasted from the rule of Tarquinius Priscus, which began in 616 BC, to the expulsion of the Etruscans in 510 BC, and most archaeologists would probably accept this. Others, however, including Gjerstad himself, see the Etruscans as having arrived in the second half of the 6th century BC and remaining in Rome until about 450 BC. It is true that throughout the first part of the 5th century BC there is evidence of continued Etruscan influence at Rome, which does not wholly fit with the traditional account of the expulsion of the Etruscan king, Lucius Tarquinius Superbus, in 510 BC and the subsequent establishment of the Roman Republic. But, as others have argued, even with their new political independence the Romans remained part of a world in which the Etruscans continued to be a major force, and it is therefore not surprising that Etruscan culture should have continued to exert its influence. Even during the regal period Rome had probably been ruled by a non-Etruscan without any lessening of Etruscan cultural impact. Tarquinius Priscus, the first Etruscan king of Rome, was succeeded by Servius Tullius, who, according to a Roman tradition accepted by most scholars, was a Latin by birth. The story explaining his succession is not a very convincing one, combining a divine conception (his mother was made pregnant by a flame) with a typically dubious piece of etymology – the name Servius was related to the fact that when his mother was captured by the Etruscans in the siege of her native city of Corniculum she was made a slave or *serva*. But although the first Etruscologist, the Emperor Claudius, later tried to identify Servius with an Etruscan adventurer named Macstarna (itself a Latin word related to *magister*), the traditional belief in his Latin origins was probably justified, and demonstrates that Etruscan influence could continue even under a Latin king. In any case it is clear that for about a century the Etruscans retained their prominence in Rome, and the immense changes which they produced left a permanent mark on both the city and her inhabitants.

Indeed it is probably true to say that the city of Rome did not so much grow under the Etruscans as come into being, since it is hardly possible to think in urban terms of the earlier groups of wattle-and-daub huts, spread out over the hills. The drainage of the entire area of the Forum Romanum, made possible by superior Etruscan technology, converted it into the center of the new city. The graves and huts of earlier days were filled in or knocked down and a pebbled pavement was laid down; rectangular houses roofed with tiles were constructed, with walls of mud-brick covered with painted stucco. Temples and shrines were built, the most famous of which was the temple to Jupiter Optimus Maximus on the Capitoline, a building of imposing splendor which according to tradition was begun by the first Etruscan king of Rome, Tarquinius Priscus, almost finished in the reign of the last one, Tarquinius Superbus, and finally dedicated for the first time in the first year of the Republic. Clearly it was important to the Romans' *amour propre* that their most important temple should not have been inaugurated under Etruscan rule, but everything about it was Etruscan in inspiration: the division of the cult chamber into three parts is characteristic of Etruscan temple architecture, and the famous Etruscan sculptor Vulca was summoned from Veii to produce the statue of Jupiter that was to be placed in the central *cella*. Later restorations and reconstructions of the temple have left little remaining of the original structure, but the discovery of large quantities of terracotta decorations in excavations of a few years ago around the church of Sant' Omobono in the area of the Forum

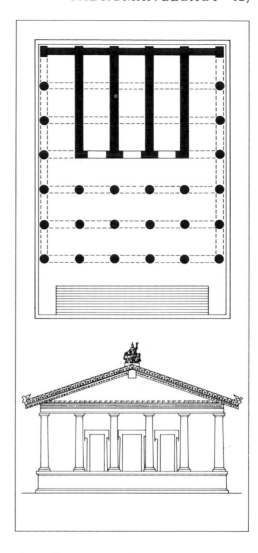

Plan and reconstruction of the Temple of Capitoline Jupiter, begun, according to the traditional account, by Tarquinius Priscus and finally dedicated shortly after the foundation of the Roman Republic in 509 BC. In this reconstruction the foundation of the temple measured 51 × 74 m, with a column diameter of 2 m. The building was destroyed and restored many times in Roman history.

Boarium, which are probably from two slightly later temples, those of Fortuna and of Mater Matuta, has helped in reconstructing its probable appearance. In size and in richness the Temple of Jupiter could compare not only with other buildings elsewhere in Etruria, but with contemporary Greek temples also, and the construction of so elaborate a structure in Rome gives some measure of the effects of Etruscan occupation.

But at the same time that it illustrates the new skills in architectural construction and decoration that were imported into Rome, the temple marks a new stage in the development of Roman thought, and one that brought the Romans for the first time into the mainstream of Mediterranean culture. In the pre-Etruscan period, as far as we can tell, the religious powers revered by the Romans were forces of nature as much as individually conceived deities, and were seldom if ever represented in the form of images. Where an image did exist in early Italic religion it took the form of an object, and not a human shape; thus Mars was represented by a spear, and Vesta the goddess of the hearth by fire, which remained her symbol even in later times. The whole complicated apparatus of Greek tradition, with the Olympian gods, their lives and loves and personal interference in human affairs, all envisaged in anthropomorphic terms, finds no counterpart in early Italic religion. The arrival of the Etruscans saw the introduction into Rome of the eastern Mediterranean tradition, filtered through Etruscan sensibilities, of gods who were both imagined and actually depicted in individual human terms. Vulca's statue of Jupiter, therefore, represented literally a new way of looking at a god, and at the same time replaced, as the central focus of Roman religion, the rough fertility figure of Mars with a version of the Greek Zeus, a fatherly symbol of supreme power. This demotion of Mars was accompanied by a process whereby he and other traditional Latin gods began to be equated with Etruscan and Greek deities and represented in the same way. The significance of this change and its effect upon Roman religion was immense, and over the succeeding centuries ancient Latin deities, at first through Etruscan intermediaries, became more and more identified with Greek gods, often losing their original significance under their new name and form. At the end of the 3rd century BC, when Rome became increasingly exposed to Greek ideas, the degree of assimilation became even more marked, and the process of Hellenization is especially evident in Roman art – which for the 3rd and 2nd centuries BC means art brought to Rome as much as art produced there. It is certainly easier to create and identify with figures who have recognizable human characteristics – Venus as the model of feminine sensual beauty, for example, or the lame but vigorous smith Vulcan – than it is to produce works of art using fire or spears as subjects, and it is difficult to imagine how the Romans of the late Republic and early Empire could have adopted Greek styles and techniques without also adopting their subject matter and iconography.

But the Italic tradition of faith in abstract concepts which were related to a simpler stage of life was not abandoned and their literature shows that the Romans continued to revere deities who, even though they rarely if ever appear in public works of art, were probably closer to the hearts of the average citizen. Each Roman's house was protected by its own Lares, or household gods, whose images were placed in a small shrine or sometimes in a little room known as the Lararium. The custom was probably related to the Etruscan cult of Laran or Lalan, but it may well be Italic in origin, and an appeal to the Lares of the city was included, as we saw, in the hymn of

Above: The introduction of games into Rome is traditionally attributed to the Etruscans, who often depicted sporting occasions in their tomb painting. This example comes from the Tomb of the Monkey at Chiusi.

Top: By the time of the later Empire, the Roman taste for violence had created a demand for the kind of gladiatorial spectacle represented in this famous mosaic, now in the Villa Borghese, Rome. Contests between men and men, and men and animals are both represented. This particular example dates to the mid-3rd century AD.

the Arval Brothers. Other guardian spirits also watched over the home: Carden, the goddess of the hinge, Limentinus, god of the threshold, and Forculus, god of the door. The countryman revered other forces. Epona was the protecting goddess of horses and asses while Bubona watched over cattle. In some cases the Romans' conception of these spirits was so vague that they can take on either male or female form; thus the power that averted rust or mildew was known as either the god Robigus or the goddess Robigo, whose festival, the Robigalia, was celebrated annually on 25 April.

These naive irrational forces are a long way from the Greek tradition of recognizable human characteristics rationalized in divine form; they lack entirely the intellectual satisfaction and the sophistication of the Greek gods, whose complex behavior provides a commentary on, if not an explanation of, human existence. But there is no doubt that many Romans took them seriously, and their cults continued well into the Empire, in some cases even surviving the introduction of Christianity as the state religion in 324 AD. It is often said that the official Roman religion had little to offer to its citizens in terms of spiritual comfort or answers to the problems of existence, and this is probably true for those Romans whose intellectual or philosophical tastes were too sophisticated to allow them to derive much comfort from a belief in such simple deities – it is difficult to imagine a Marcus Aurelius, for example, displaying much enthusiasm for the god of mildew. Throughout their history the Romans were surprisingly open to new ideas and religions, and a lack of satisfaction with their own native deities probably explains their tolerance of, indeed enthusiasm for, a wide array of foreign cults whose appeal lay in their elaborate rituals and promise of bliss in a future life. But at a level below that of statesmen and thinkers, the old beliefs continued to retain their power, and the personalized deities first introduced by the Etruscans, instead of replacing them, came to represent an additional level of belief,

𐤀	A
𐤁	B
𐤂	C
𐤃	D
𐤄	E
𐤅	V
𐤆	Z
𐤇	H
𐤈	Th
𐤉	I
𐤊	K
𐤋	L
𐤌	M
𐤍	N
𐤎	(S)
𐤏	O
𐤐	P
𐤑	Ś
𐤒	Q
𐤓	R
𐤔	S
𐤕	T
𐤖	U
𐤗	Ṡ
𐤘	(Ph)
𐤙	(Ch)

The Etruscan alphabet, with a transcription of the phonetic values of the letters.

one more aesthetically attractive but perhaps less appealing to the Italian temperament.

Meanwhile, besides a new way of thinking about the gods, the Etruscans were importing other new customs into Rome. The Etruscan tradition of holding games, which is shown in a number of their tomb paintings, was probably introduced during the reigns of the Etruscan kings, who were said to have been the first to build wooden stands for the spectators at sporting events. Although the sport of chariot racing was to become one of the most typical of Roman pastimes, and centuries later was transferred to Constantinople, Constantine's New Rome in the east, its origins at Rome are almost certainly Etruscan, and the Roman Circus with its *metae*, or posts, set at each end of the racetrack to mark the turning point, and the central *spina*, is based on Etruscan models. Presumably like later Roman emperors the Etruscan kings saw the games as a way of distracting the populace from more depressing matters, while winning popularity for themselves.

Most of all, however, the period of Etruscan domination must have enlarged the Romans' way of looking at themselves and the world around. From being simple villagers living in small communities governed by tribal chiefs, they found themselves part of a large cultural unit with links throughout Italy and abroad. New roads and buildings, the superior technological level of the Etruscans as represented in achievements like the draining of the Forum, the foreign ideas and images introduced by means of imported Greek and Phoenician works of art, all these revealed possibilities that the first Romans had never dreamed of. Under Etruscan instruction new crafts developed and guilds were established, including those of the bronze workers, goldsmiths, carpenters, dyers and potters. The Etruscan symbols of authority, the magistrate's throne and the *fasces* (a bundle consisting of rods and an ax which represented the power to scourge or to execute), were later adopted as Roman insignia; even the Roman toga is Etruscan in origin. And another vital contribution of the Etruscans to the development of Roman civilization was the introduction of the alphabet: the characters in which this book is printed were taken by the Etruscans from the Greek alphabet and introduced in a modified form into Rome, thereby passing down to us. Almost as important, in view of later Roman history, was the adoption by the Etruscans of weapons and fighting techniques which had been developed by the Greeks, and the handing on of these to the Romans. The use of a round shield, metal armor to protect the body, and a thrusting rather than throwing spear were characteristic of a type of Greek infantry called hoplite, and by the 6th century equipment of the same kind had become common in Etruria; a century later the use of tight formations of troops equipped in this way gave Rome a distinct advantage in the wars with the neighboring Latin tribes that followed the expulsion of the Etruscans.

In view of the far-ranging effects of all these influences it is astonishing that Rome managed to retain its own identity and emerge from its contact with Etruscan culture stronger and changed but still independent. A symptom of the Romans' ability to retain their cultural individuality is shown by the fact that throughout the Etruscan period Latin as well as Etruscan was written as well as spoken at Rome, and surprisingly few Etruscan words ever became incorporated into the Latin vocabulary. Like the Picenes, the Umbrians and other Italic tribes the Romans managed to absorb many of the new techniques and more superficial characteristics of cultures that were in advance of them, while retaining their own character. Where the Romans were different from their neighbors was in their urge to use these advances not only to improve their own way of life, but as a means of increasing their control over others. When all is said and done no single satisfactory explanation can be given for why the Romans, unlike the other Latin peoples or the Samnites or any other contemporary culture for that matter, were driven (or, as they would have put it, inspired) to undertake massive conquests, first in Italy and then throughout the Mediterranean; we are forced to resort to such terms as "temperament" or "national character," which only express the problem in different ways. Whatever the cause, in any case, the end of Etruscan domination and the subsequent weakening of Etruscan cultural influence saw the beginning of Roman domination first of her Latin neighbors and, by the 3rd century BC, of the whole of Italy.

Republican Rome. The story of the gradual rise to power of Republican Rome and her external and internal conflicts on the way is far too involved to be described here, and in any case we are primarily concerned with the Romans as one of the many peoples of early Italy rather than as the future masters of the world. Yet it may be worthwhile to take a final look at them as they start off on their self-appointed mission to "rule the world, show mercy to the defeated and strike down the proud," as Virgil tactfully describes it. Who were these new Romans, with their combination of sturdy Latin peasant stock and urbane Etruscan culture?

For the Romans themselves both aspects of their development were significant, and if they never lost their admiration for the simple virtues and plain life-style of their ancestors they were nevertheless aware of the fact that from now on they would need to demonstrate a growing internationalism. One of the results of this conflict of cultural direction is that Rome acquired two separate foundation stories and two founding fathers, Romulus and Aeneas. The story of Romulus, although its origins cannot be traced, is almost certainly the more ancient of the two, and in its simplest form, without the accretions of later centuries, it seems an appropriate invention for the first Roman farmers. Many of the ingredients of the tale seem associated with the early days of Rome – Romulus and Remus, the twin sons of Mars, their mother Rhea Silvia murdered by her jealous uncle and they themselves subsequently miraculously saved and suckled by a she-wolf in a cave on the Palatine hill, where they were discovered by the shepherd Faustulus. It certainly became subject to considerable later elaboration, particularly at the time of the wars against the Samnites, but in its essence it relates Rome to a simple rustic Italian past.

Post-Etruscan Rome, however, needed a more noble pedigree and if possible one that connected her with the venerable world of the eastern Mediterranean; and the Greek legend of Aeneas, the Trojan prince who fled from the ruins of his burning city to found a new home in the west, provided a perfect solution. The theme of Aeneas' flight from Troy was already known in Italy from its appearance on Greek vases imported from Athens, and a cult seems to have been established in his honor at Veii at the very end of the 6th century BC, to judge from the discovery there of a group of terracotta votive statuettes, just at the time that the Romans were themselves preparing to adopt him as their founder. It is not clear whether the story of Aeneas arrived in Italy directly from Greece or was transmitted through the Greek cities of southern Italy and Sicily, but within only a few

Above: Bronze of an Etruscan warrior. British Museum. The armor is of the kind carried by Greek hoplites.

Top: Mosaic from the villa at Piazza Armerina, Sicily, early 4th century AD. These "bikini" girls from the end of the Roman Empire seem very different in spirit from the bloody contestants of almost 1,000 years earlier, although they represent the final stages of the same tradition.

Relief from the Ara Pacis, Rome. 13–9 BC. The figure to the right of center is Aeneas, who is performing a sacrifice shortly after his arrival in Italy: note the small Lararium in the top left-hand corner. The emphasis on agricultural plenty, represented by the richness of the sacrifice, is typically Augustan.

years the Greeks themselves were prepared to accept the new Roman version of events. Around 450 BC the Greek historian Hellanicus wrote that "Aeneas came from the country of the Molossians and founded Rome," and even provided a characteristically fanciful explanation for the city's name: Aeneas had been accompanied on his voyage there by a Trojan woman called Rhome. There remained the problem that according to their own chronology the Romans were faced with a gap of some 500 years between the arrival of Aeneas and the traditional date of the founding of the city, but this was solved by the invention of a line of kings, one of the last of whom was the father of Rhea Silvia, the mother of Romulus and Remus.

In this way Rome could take her place among the other Mediterranean powers with an appropriately impressive explanation of her origins, and one that linked her to the whole Greek epic tradition. And there are signs that from the earliest days of the Republic Roman power was already being taken seriously both inside and outside Italy. If we can believe a document quoted by the 2nd-century BC Greek historian Polybius, the Carthaginians signed a treaty with the new Republic in its first year, in which the Romans apparently claimed sovereignty over a number of neighboring cities and "any other Latin peoples who are subject to Rome." The treaty, if we accept it as genuine, was probably a renewal of one previously existing between the Carthaginians and Etruscan Rome, and it is a tribute to Rome's new standing that Carthage should have hastened to establish bonds of friendship with the young state and have accepted Roman domination of a sizable portion of Latium. That domination was challenged by the Latins themselves in the following years, but in 496 BC a decisive battle at Lake Regillus reestablished Rome as the leading power in Latium, and a treaty was signed according to which the peace between Romans and Latins should last "as long as heaven and earth remain in their places." In view of the events which had preceded it, this must have seemed a rather optimistic hope, but it lasted long enough at any rate to allow Rome together with the Latins to face the Aequi, the Volsci and the Sabines, and prepare for the eventual struggle with the Etruscans.

The following centuries saw the growing Roman domination of Italy and the defeat of her rivals abroad, and in the process political and military affairs took precedence over the arts and literature. By the time the Romans could afford to relax again they were soon overwhelmed intellectually and artistically by the ideas of the later stages of Greek culture which are known as Hellenistic. From the 3rd century BC most Roman works of art followed Greek models for their form and content: Roman plays were based on Greek originals, Roman temples imitated at least in part Greek buildings, and Roman sculpture and painting depicted episodes from Greek mythology. But although the influence of Greek thought was profound and long lasting, behind it and often buried beneath it there can still be seen the effects of Rome's Italian past. Their own consciousness of their origins often took the form of a nostalgia for a life of rustic simplicity which had become sadly lost in the complicated world of imperial realities. Virgil, who in the *Aeneid* produced perhaps the most elaborate of all Roman literary assimilations of Greek form and technique, is at the same time among the most Italian of poets when in his poem on farming, the *Georgics*, he contrasts the corruptions of politics and the Forum with life in the country: "The happiest of men, if only they knew it, are the farmers:

Below right: The Capitoline She-Wolf, bronze, late 6th or early 5th century BC. Palazzo dei Conservatori, Rome. Height 75 cm, length 114 cm. The twins, Romulus and Remus, were added in the Renaissance. Although either this statue or one very like it became the mascot of Rome, and was dedicated on the Capitoline in 296 BC, its origin is Etruscan. The tension and power are reminiscent of the Chimaera of Arezzo, although their effect is somewhat diminished by the chubby twins.

Below: Terracotta statuette of Aeneas carrying his father Anchises on his back, from Veii, mid-5th century BC. Villa Giulia, Rome.

Above: Section of the wall decoration from the underground grotto chamber in the Villa of Prima Porta, just to the north of Rome, c. 30–25 BC. Museo Nazionale, Rome. Height of the frescoes 3 m. The entire room represents a garden, with trees planted behind low fences. In the foreground are rose bushes, pomegranate trees and birds. The effect of depth and care for detail are beautifully rendered.

Opposite: The Roman interest in landscape and love of the outdoors are shown in this painting from Pompeii in which Pan and his attendant nymphs are inserted into an open-air scene.

far from the noise of conflict they find true justice in the earth which so freely offers up its bounty. No houses pouring out crowds of visitors from every door, no tortoiseshell inlays for them to gape at, nor gold embroidery nor Corinthian bronzes . . . the farmer plows his earth and by his annual work supports home and family, flocks and herds. With no pause the year brings its bounty of apples, then new-born lambs, and fields full of corn produce loaded barns. Winter comes: time to press the olives, while the pigs come home happy, stuffed with acorns. Autumn too has its rewards: on the high rocky slopes the vines bask in the warmth, and meanwhile the farmer's children hang around him for kisses, at home all is simple and pure, the cows are heavy with rich milk and he himself can take a rest stretched out on the grass . . . that is how once the Sabines of olden days used to live, and Remus and his brother; that is surely how Etruria grew strong and Rome became the most beautiful city in the world, in the day when a single wall could enclose every one of her hills." The note of regret is genuine and touching, even though it was to become a commonplace of Latin literary expression.

In the visual arts it is much more difficult to isolate the Italic elements in the later Roman tradition, partly because, as we have seen, so much art produced in Italy was itself directly influenced by Greek ideas, and partly because its influence was confined to a relatively early stage in the development of Roman styles and tastes. By the 2nd century BC the years of fighting against the spread of Roman power had finally demoralized the Etruscan and Italic peoples, and little original local art was being produced anywhere except in the south. We saw the effects of this pessimism in the Etruscan tomb paintings, and elsewhere in Italy the sense of hopelessness

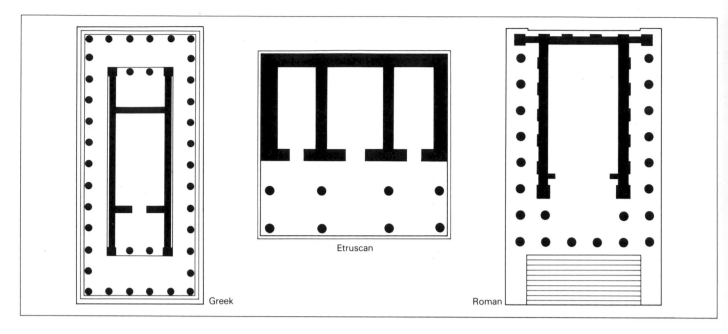

The form of the Roman temple is the result of combining Greek and Etruscan types. The surrounding colonnade (at the back represented by pilasters) and the single cella were borrowed from the Greeks, while the high podium, approached by a long flight of steps, and the deep portico are characteristically Etruscan.

and the growing loss of a personal identity produced works that in their crudeness of workmanship seem to reject any tradition, Greek, Etruscan or even their own. The crudely carved heads found in the cemeteries of Benevento and Taranto seem an aptly gloomy reflection of the world of their creators. Nor was there any demand at Rome itself for Italian art, since the Roman conquest of Greece had been followed by the carrying off to Rome and elsewhere in Italy as booty large numbers of Hellenistic works of art which served to form the tastes of the connoisseurs of the late Republic in both the capital and the provinces. Even Augustus' attempt to encourage the rebirth of local pride in the Italian towns did little to foster the development of Italic art. Its contribution, therefore, to Roman art consisted generally of those ideas which had been taken by the Romans in earlier times, and then combined with Greek elements. In town-planning, for example, both Greek and Etruscan ideas seem to have influenced the development of Roman systems of urban organization. Indeed the Etruscans' use of long rectangular city blocks with streets intersecting at right angles, found at Etruscan sites like Marzabotto and Capua, was probably itself learned from the Greek colonies of southern Italy, although the formal requirements of the Etruscan city, often dictated by religious considerations, do seem to have made their mark on Roman towns. Similarly, the Roman temple combines features of both Greek and Etruscan temple designs, while the form of Roman houses – at least as seen at Pompeii – has Samnite precedents.

It used to be the fashion to regard Roman art as wholly derived from Greek models, a provincial version of Hellenistic culture with no originality of its own. An exploration of the world of her predecessors and contemporaries in Italy, if it does nothing else, should serve to demonstrate that Etruscans, Umbrians, Samnites and others played their part too in forming Roman style, and in the future a growing understanding of these other peoples of Italy may help to identify their contribution more exactly. But paradoxically the more their influence is perceived, the less unoriginal Roman art seems: as in other aspects of their culture, the Romans' power of assimilation, far from representing a weakness on their part, was among their greatest assets.

FURTHER READING

PREHISTORIC ITALY
Barfield, L., *Northern Italy before Rome* (London, 1971).
Brea, L. B., *Sicily before the Greeks* (London, 1966).
Guido, M., *Sardinia* (London, 1963).
Trump, D. H., *Central and Southern Italy before Rome* (London, 1965).

VILLANOVANS AND ETRUSCANS
Banti, L., *The Etruscan Cities and their Culture* (London, 1973).
Brown, W. L., *The Etruscan Lion* (Oxford, 1960).
Coarelli, F. (ed.), *Etruscan Cities* (London, 1975).
Hencken, H., *Tarquinia, Villanovans and Early Etruscans* (Cambridge, Mass., 1968).
Heurgon, J., *La Vie quotidienne chez les étrusques* (Paris, 1961).
Pallottino, M., *The Etruscans* (London, 1974).
Richardson, E., *The Etruscans: Their Art and Culture* (London, 1976).
Scullard, H. H., *The Etruscan Cities and Rome* (London, 1967).

EARLY ROME
Alföldi, A., *Early Rome and the Latins* (Ann Arbor, Mich., 1965).
Galinsky, G. K., *Aeneas, Sicily and Rome* (Princeton, N.J., 1969).
Gjerstad, E., *Early Rome*, 6 vols. (Lund, 1953–73).
Harris, W. V., *Rome in Etruria and Umbria* (Oxford, 1971).
Heurgon, J., *The Rise of Rome, to 264 BC* (London, 1973).
Müller-Karpe, H., *Zur Stadtwerdung Roms* (Heidelberg, 1962).

FOREIGNERS IN ITALY
Boardman, J., *The Greeks Overseas* (Harmondsworth, 1964).
Dunbabin, T. J., *The Western Greeks* (Oxford, 1948).
Harden, D., *The Phoenicians* (Harmondsworth, 1971).
Ross Holloway, R., *Influences and Styles in the Late Archaic and Early Classical Greek Sculpture of Sicily and Magna Graecia* (Louvain, 1975).
Taylour, W., *Mycenaean Pottery in Italy and Adjacent Areas* (Cambridge, 1958).
Woodhead, A. G., *The Greeks in the West* (London, 1962).

ART IN EARLY ITALY
Bianchi Bandinelli, R., and A. Giuliano, *Les Etrusques et l'Italie avant Rome* (Paris, 1973).
Beazley, J., *Etruscan Vase Painting* (Oxford, 1947).
Boethius, A., and J. B. Ward-Perkins, *Etruscan and Roman Architecture* (Harmondsworth, 1970).
Bonfante, L., *Etruscan Dress* (London, 1975).
Haynes, S., *Etruscan Sculpture* (London, 1975).
Napoli, M., *La Tomba del Tuffatore* (Bari, 1970).
Pallottino, M., *Civiltà artistica etrusco-italica* (Florence, 1971).
Randall-MacIver, D., *The Iron Age in Italy* (Oxford, 1927).
Richter, G. M. A., *Ancient Italy* (Ann Arbor, Mich., 1955).

ACKNOWLEDGMENTS

Unless otherwise stated all the illustrations on a given page are credited to the same source.

ADAGP, Paris; photo Galerie Maeght, Paris 49

Alinari, Florence 46 (top)

Ashmolean Museum, Oxford (Courtesy National Museum of Wales) 103 (bottom)

Badisches Landesmuseum, Karlsruhe 59

Bibliothèque Nationale, Paris 79 (bottom)

Bildarchiv Preussischer Kulturbesitz, W. Berlin 36 (left)

John Brennan, Oxford 130, Glossary

Stephen Cocking, Oxford 13, 17 (top), 19 (top left), 26 (bottom), 57, 61 (bottom), 120 (left), 127, 136

Fotocielo, Rome 27 (top right), 47

Fotomas Index, London 45

John Fuller, Cambridge 14, 15 (bottom), 16 (bottom right), 17 (bottom), 19 (bottom left), 20, 54, 62 (bottom), 73 (top left and top right), 75 (top right), 111, 126

Mario Gerardi Fotografo, Rome 21, 114

Sonia Halliday Photographs, Weston Turville 18 (top)

Robert Harding Associates, London 15 (top), 84 (left)

Hirmer Verlag, Munich 40, 66, 82, 92, 94 (bottom), 95, 96 (bottom), 133 (right)

Michael Holford Library, Loughton 9, 23 (right), 31, 51 (bottom and right), 52 (bottom), 77, 78, 83 (bottom), 84 (right), 112

Lovell Johns, Oxford 11, 12 (right), 18 (bottom), 27 (top left), 55, 76, 100, 124 (left)

Mansell Collection, London 32, 35, 86 (bottom)

Metropolitan Museum of Art, New York 64 (bottom)

Musée de l'Homme, Paris 12 (left)

Nationalmuseet, Copenhagen 28 (bottom left)

Phaidon Press, Oxford Frontispiece, 53 (bottom), 87, 89, 103 (top)

Mauro Pucciarelli, Rome 34 (bottom), 39, 81 (left), 95 (bottom), 96 (top left), 99, 119 (bottom left), 124 (bottom), 128 (bottom), 131 (bottom), 132

Radio Times Hulton Picture Library, London 44

Rhode Island School of Design, Providence, Museum of Art, Mary B. Jackson Fund 72 (top)

David Ridgway, Edinburgh 26 (top), 27 (bottom left)

Rome University, Instituto di Etruscologia e Antichità Italiche, in M. Pallottino, *The Etruscans*, London 1974, 79 (top)

Royal Collection, Windsor (Copyright reserved) 30

Scala, Florence 16 (left and top right), 19 (right), 22, 23 (left), 27 (bottom right), 28 (bottom right), 29 (top left and bottom), 34 (top), 35 (top), 36 (right), 37, 38, 42, 43, 50 (top), 51 (top and center left), 52 (top), 53 (top and center), 61 (top), 62 (top), 63, 65, 70, 71, 72 (bottom), 73 (bottom left, center left and bottom right), 74, 75 (top right, bottom left and bottom center), 80, 81 (right), 83 (top), 85, 86, 90, 91, 93, 94 (top), 96 (top right), 97, 104, 105 (top), 107, 109, 110, 113, 115, 116, 117, 118, 119, 120 (bottom and right), 121 (right, center and bottom), 123, 128 (top), 131, 134, 135

Edwin Smith, Saffron Walden 28 (top), 29 (top right), 105 (bottom), 124 (top right)

Henri Stierlin, Geneva 46 (bottom)

Leonard von Matt, Buochs 48, 68, 69, 133 (left)

Yale University Art Gallery, New Haven, Conn., Gift of Memory of Ward Cheney, B.A. 1922, 64 (top)

The Publishers have attempted to observe the legal requirements with respect to the rights of the suppliers of photographic materials. Nevertheless, persons who have claims are invited to apply to the Publishers.

GLOSSARY

Aedile Roman magistrate whose duties included the control of weights and measures, the care of streets and buildings, and the guardianship of public order and decency. The Samnite equivalent was the Aidilis.

Aeneid Epic poem by **Virgil** which describes in 12 books the wanderings of the Trojan prince Aeneas: after fleeing from Troy, Aeneas finally arrives in Italy, where he founds a new Troy in Latium.

Aeolian Islands Group of small islands of volcanic origin which lie off the northeast coast of Sicily. In recent years several **Neolithic** sites have been excavated on them, as well as late **Bronze Age** settlements. The most important are on Lipari (where there is also an excellent museum), Filicudi and Panarea.

Aeschylus (c. 525–456 BC) Greek tragic poet, seven of whose plays survive. He twice visited Sicily, attracted there by the wealth and culture to be found at the court of **Hieron** of Syracuse, for whom he wrote his play *The Women of Etna* (now lost). After returning to Athens, he came back to Sicily in 458 BC, where he died near Gela: according to one story he was killed by an eagle dropping a tortoise on his bare head.

Aeschylus

Alexandria City on the coast of Egypt which became the intellectual and literary center of the Greek world after the fall of Athens. It was the capital of the Egypt of the Ptolemies, the first of whom, Ptolemy Soter (366–283 BC), founded there the famous Library and Museum.

Anatolia Area of the Near East which corresponds to modern Turkey, immensely rich in archaeological material from the **Paleolithic** to the Roman periods.

Annio of Viterbo (1432–1502) Dominican monk, whose enthusiasm for the Etruscans led him to forge a number of inscriptions. His chief work, *Commentaria super opera diversorum auctorum de antiquitatibus loquentium*, was published at Rome in 1498, and includes supposed quotations from ancient authors which he invented himself.

Apennine culture Name given to the predominant culture of central and southern Italy during the **Bronze Age**, although in fact the Apennine people rarely used bronze. They were primarily farmers and stockbreeders, although there is some evidence of trade. In general they buried rather than cremated their dead.

Aramaic Northern branch of the Semitic family of languages, written in the **Phoenician** script, commonly spoken in the Near East during the Iron Age.

Archilochus (c. 680–640 BC) Greek lyric poet, born in Paros, of whose work only a few fragments survive. His poems seem to have been characterized by a spirit of sharp satire and bitter mockery. Archilochus is one of the ancient writers used as a source by **Annio of Viterbo**, who forged a number of additional fragments which he tried to pass off as genuine.

Ariadne In Greek mythology the daughter of King Minos of **Knossos** who fell in love with Theseus when he came to Crete to kill the Minotaur. Having helped Theseus to leave the labyrinth after killing the monster, she left Crete with him, only to be deserted and left on the island of Naxos. Here she was found by the young god **Dionysus**, who made her his bride – an episode popular with artists of later ages and with composers from Monteverdi to Richard Strauss.

Ash urns (sometimes known as cinerary urns) General term for receptacles which were used to contain the bones and ashes of the dead after cremation. Different cultures used different forms of urn: see **Biconical, Canopic, Hut-urns** below.

Astarte Chief female deity of the **Phoenicians**, who combined the role of mother and fertility goddess, and was known to the **Carthaginians** as Tanit. In general she was equated with the Greek goddess Aphrodite (the goddess of physical love), but sometimes became identified with the eastern mother-goddess Cybele, and (especially in the west) with Hera, or Roman Juno. In the **Pyrgi tablets**, found in the late 6th-century BC temple dedicated to her, she is linked with the Etruscan goddess **Uni**.

Augustus (63 BC–14 AD) First Roman emperor, whose assumption of power dates in practice to 31 BC, following his defeat of Antony and Cleopatra at the battle of Actium, although his position was formalized in 27 BC. As an imperial patron of the arts, he encouraged writers like **Virgil** and Horace, while initiating a massive new building program at Rome and in the provinces. As part of his emphasis on peace and a return to the simple life, he stressed the virtues of Rome's Italian pastoral origins.

Balearic Islands Group of islands off the east coast of Spain, of which the chief ones are Majorca, Minorca and Ibiza. The peoples of the **Bronze Age** there seem to have had links with the contemporary culture of Sardinia, and they served as a link between Spain and the eastern Mediterranean.

Bandinelli, Baccio (1493–1560) Florentine sculptor, much of whose work shows the typical Renaissance preoccupation with Classical themes and styles, and whose copy of the **Laocoön** was brought to Florence where it helped to create an interest in ancient art.

Beaker Kind of deep drinking vessel, often found buried with the dead, which seems to have originated around 2000 BC in northern and western Europe and spread eastwards. Examples of a kind found in the Pyrenees and southwest France have been found in Sardinia: they date to the early second millennium BC.

Bianchi Bandinelli, Ranuccio (1900–75)

Distinguished Italian archaeologist, who has played an important part in the reassessment of Etruscan and Roman art, and their connections with the art of their contemporaries in Italy. In the years immediately following World War II he was in charge of reorganizing Italy's museums and damaged monuments.

Biconical urns Type of **ash urn** commonly found in Villanovan graves: the base narrows to a foot and the urns are often covered with a lid that rises to a blunt point, suggesting the shape of two cones joined at their mouths.

Bronze Age In mainland Italy the introduction of bronze occurred around 1800 BC, although techniques of bronze working had arrived in Sicily somewhat earlier, around 2000 BC. The first culture to make significant use of bronze, however, was that of the **Terramara** people, about 1500 BC. The Bronze Age began to die out at the end of the second millennium BC, as new techniques of iron working made their way westwards, but bronze continued to be an important commodity for early **Iron Age** people like the Villanovans.

Bucchero Type of Etruscan pottery common from the 8th to the 4th centuries BC, black or gray in color with a glossy finish: there are two varieties, *bucchero pesante* (with thick walls) and *bucchero sottile* (with thin walls). The vessels are often decorated with designs molded or applied in relief, and occasionally with impressions produced by cylinder seals. The imaginative way in which the shapes of the vessels are often varied, the use of applied three-dimensional decoration, and the absence of painted designs or figures all contrast strongly with contemporary Greek pottery styles.

Caeretan hydriai Group of about 30 *hydriai*, or water jugs, most of which were found at Cerveteri (the Latin name of which is Caere). They date to the late 6th century BC and are all the product of a single workshop, if not a single artist. Most scholars believe that they were produced in Cerveteri itself by immigrant Greek artists, although some have claimed that they were imported from Asia Minor.

Candelabrum Bronze candleholder consisting of a vertical rod standing on a tripod, at the top of which extend horizontal arms to which candles or torches were fixed. There is often a decorative figure or other ornament at the center between the arms.

Canopic urns Type of **ash urn** found at Chiusi, in which the lid takes the form of a human head, perhaps representing the deceased. In some cases the body of the urn is also given human features – arms and hands – and a number of examples were placed on chairs with rounded backs. The name Canopic

is derived from the Canopic urns of Egypt, used to contain the internal organs of the mummified dead, which bore on their lids portraits of the divinities associated with the individual organs. In the case of the Etruscan urns, however, the heads almost certainly have no connection with deities.

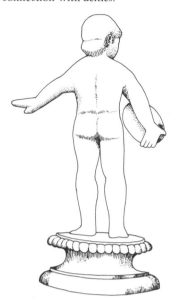

Bronze end-figure to a candelabrum

Carthage Phoenician colony founded on the coast of North Africa (8 miles from modern Tunis) in 814 BC. When the Phoenicians were conquered by Nebuchadnezzar in 574 BC, and subsequently absorbed into the Persian empire when Babylon was defeated in 539 BC, the Carthaginians established themselves as an independent power in the west. Their trade rivalry with the Greeks and the Etruscans produced a series of conflicts throughout the 6th and 5th centuries BC, and they were finally defeated by Rome at the end of the Second **Punic war** in 202 BC. Although subsequently no longer any threat, Carthage was razed to the ground by the Romans in 146 BC.

Carved grave slab from Castelluccio

Castelluccio Site of a **necropolis** in eastern Sicily which has given its name to an Early Bronze Age culture there. Among its most characteristic products are a series of bossed bone plaques which have been compared to similar objects found in Greece dating to the same period, suggesting links with the eastern Mediterranean.

Cato, Marcus Porcius (234–149 BC) Roman statesman and historian, famous for the austerity of his manner. Among his works was a handbook on farming, *De Re Rustica*, which survives, and the *Origins*, a lost work on the history of the Romans and the other peoples of Italy, parts of which were "discovered" (that is to say invented) by **Annio of Viterbo**.

Cella Inner closed part of a temple which housed the cult statue of the deity.

Cellini, Benvenuto (1500–71) Florentine sculptor and goldsmith, well known also for his lively autobiography. He was responsible for repairing the Chimaera of Arezzo and providing it with left front and back feet, the originals of which were missing.

Chamber tomb Tomb consisting of a room either constructed of stone or cut into a natural rock face which often served for a series of burials over a period of time.

Interior of a chamber tomb at Monterozzi

Charon (Greek), **Charun** or **Charu** (Etruscan) Although associated with the underworld in both Greek and Etruscan mythology, the two figures differ in their character and depiction. The Greek Charon is the grim, taciturn ferryman who rows the souls of the dead across the river of the underworld to Hades, while the Etruscan Charun is portrayed as a ferocious demon, generally armed with a hammer, who torments and tortures the dead upon their arrival there.

Cist Box of cylindrical shape, made of metal (occasionally of wood faced with metal), and covered by a lid which often has small human figures or other decoration on it. *Cistae* are often decorated with engraved designs which

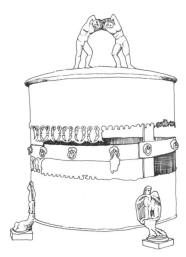

Bronze cist from Praeneste

as in the case of the famous Ficoroni cist, are of mythological subjects.

Claudius (10 BC–54 AD) Roman emperor 41–54 AD. A scholar who unexpectedly became emperor, his works (all almost entirely lost) included a History of the Etruscans, a History of Carthage and an Autobiography. Among his interests was grammar, and during his reign he added three letters to the Latin alphabet, the use of which, however, barely survived his reign.

Constantine (272–337 AD) Junior emperor in the west from 306, and later (324) sole ruler of the Roman world, he established Christianity as the official state religion, and moved the capital of the empire from Rome to Byzantium, which he renamed Constantinople.

Consualia Festival of an ancient Italian earth god, Consus, the celebration of which was related to harvest rituals. It was held twice a year at Rome, on 21 August after the harvest itself and on 15 December after the sowing of the crops for the following year. According to tradition the festival had been initiated by **Romulus**, and at its first celebration the Rape of the Sabine Women took place.

Corbeling System of roofing stone chambers which uses courses of stone, each one of which overhangs the one beneath until the hole at the top is small enough to be covered by a single stone. In this way the weight presses downwards and there is no need for a keystone to control lateral stress. The most famous examples in the Mediterranean are to be found in Greece (the **Mycenaean** so-called beehive tombs) but the same principle of construction is often used in the **Nuraghi** of Sardinia.

Cyclades Group of islands in the central Aegean, off the east coast of mainland Greece. The Cyclades were a center of culture as early

as the **Neolithic** period, when the civilization known as Cycladic produced large numbers of marble figurines, highly stylized but of great beauty of form and texture. The islands' outstanding natural supplies of marble made them a center for sculpture in the Archaic and Classical periods, two millennia later.

Delphi Sanctuary in central Greece which was one of the most sacred shrines in the Greek world and the site of a famous oracle of Apollo. The god was often consulted by foreigners as well as Greeks, many of whom maintained their own chapels and treasuries there in which were deposited gifts to the sanctuary: among these treasuries was one dedicated by Cerveteri, the only Etruscan city permanently represented at Delphi.

Dempster, Thomas (1579–1625) Scottish Etruscologist of the early 17th century. He taught at the universities of Paris, Bologna and Pisa and wrote a work on the Etruscans in seven volumes, *De Etruria Regali*. When published in Florence a century later (1723–24), this book did much to stimulate interest in Etruscan archaeology.

Dennis, George 19th-century English traveler and writer on the Etruscans, whose *Cities and Cemeteries of Etruria* first appeared in 1848, containing a description of his journeys in search of Etruscan sites and antiquities throughout central Italy, where he held a consular post. This work, the last (and best) edition of which appeared complete with revisions in 1883, combines a detailed and scholarly description of the material with a humanity and humor which are perhaps unsurpassed in the history of Etruscology. In many cases his account preserves information about objects and sites which have subsequently disappeared or been destroyed, and even when his conclusions are inevitably outdated they are still worth reading for the charm and wit with which they are presented. In addition to its other virtues, his book preserves a vivid – and sometimes horrific – description of the rigors of travel in 19th-century Etruria.

Diodorus Siculus (fl. 60–30 BC) Greek historian born in Sicily: 25 of the 40 volumes of his *Library of History* survive, a work which attempts to narrate the history of the Mediterranean world from mythological times to the age of Cicero. Although as a historian he is often inaccurate and excessively dependent on his sources, his work is valuable for the history of Sicily.

Dionysius I Ruler of Syracuse from 405 to 367 BC. Notorious for his cruelty and vindictiveness, he waged continuous and successful war against the **Carthaginians**. His brother Dion was a friend of **Plato** who paid two visits to Syracuse, the second in 367 BC to serve as tutor to Dionysius' son, Dionysius II,

who ruled from 367 to 343 BC.

Dionysius of Halicarnassus (fl. 30–8 BC) Greek writer and scholar who came to Rome as a teacher of rhetoric. His *Roman Antiquities*, written at Rome, survives in part and consisted of a long-winded and often confused account of Roman history from its earliest days to the First **Punic war**. He is chiefly famous in the history of Etruscology as the first scholar to claim that the Etruscans were autochthonous, that is native to Italy, rather than immigrants from abroad.

Dionysus Roman Bacchus. The god of fertility, especially as represented by the vine, and therefore the god of wine and the emotions. Dionysus formed the central figure of a number of cults throughout the Greco-Roman world, some of which were notorious for their orgiastic excesses: in 186 BC the Roman Senate prohibited the celebration of the Bacchanalia. He appears in Etruscan mythology as Fufluns.

Dionysus and a satyr

Dodecapolis Etruscan League of 12 Cities, probably religious rather than political in character. The members consisted of the leading 12 cities of the day, and therefore changed during the course of Etruscan history. In addition to the Dodecapolis of Etruria proper, ancient writers speak of two other leagues, one in Campania and one in northern Italy in the Po valley, but the composition of these is even more uncertain than that of the Etrurian league.

Donatello (c. 1386–1466) Florentine sculptor of the early Renaissance, some of whose works seem to show the influence of Etruscan art: famous for the intensity and immediacy of his sculptures.

Doric Greek architectural order. The earliest and the simplest of the three orders of Greek architecture (the other two are the Ionic and the Corinthian), it made little appeal to the Roman taste, although a debased form of it known as Tuscan does appear in Roman architecture.

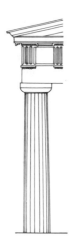

The Doric order

Eugubian tablets Seven bronze tablets found at Gubbio in 1444, bearing an inscription in Umbrian. Five of them are written in Etruscan characters and two in Latin letters.

Fasces Symbol of supreme authority in the Roman state, probably dating back to the time of the Etruscan kings. It consisted of a bundle of rods of elm or birch, enclosing an ax, the whole bundle being bound together with a red strap. It became one of the symbols of the 20th-century Italian political movement which derived its name, Fascismo, from it.

Felsina Etruscan name for Bologna.

Fibula Fastner for clothing, much like the modern safety pin. The earliest fibulae date to around 1300 BC, and a wide variety of types developed during the succeeding centuries. They were frequently used by the Etruscans, who sometimes decorated them with elaborate incrustations.

Bronze fibula from Capena

Forum Main square of a Roman town, serving as both administrative center and marketplace. At Rome itself the oldest of the fora was the Forum Romanum, center of political life, and other fora developed as markets: the Forum Boarium or cattle market, the Forum Holitorium or vegetable market, and others. Under the Empire individual emperors, including **Augustus** and Trajan, sponsored the construction of additional fora which served mainly as public monuments and reminders of imperial grandeur.

François vase One of the most famous of all Greek Archaic vases, produced around 570 BC by the potter Ergotimos and the painter Kleitias, and found in the 19th century near Chiusi. It is now in the Museo Archeologico, Florence.

Ghiberti, Lorenzo (1378–1455) Florentine sculptor and goldsmith of the early Renaissance, whose major works are the north and east doors (the latter the so-called Gates of Paradise) of the baptistery in Florence. Ghiberti was one of the first Renaissance artists to take a serious interest in collecting ancient works of art, and his collection included engraved gems as well as sculptures.

Gjerstad, Einar Contemporary Swedish archaeologist who has written a number of major, if controversial, works on the history and archaeology of early Rome.

Archaic head of the Gorgon Medusa

Gorgons According to Greek mythology three female monsters, their hair consisting of snakes, whose look turns the beholder to stone. Two of them, Stheno and Euryale, are immortal while Medusa was decapitated by Perseus, who presented the head to Athene. The Gorgon head, or Gorgoneion, was commonly used in Greek art as a decorative device, probably originally as a means of averting evil, although it later degenerated into a commonplace. In Etruscan art it is sometimes found on **Bucchero** vessels.

Hellanicus (c. 490–405 BC) Greek historian, the first writer to try to introduce a systematic chronology into the study of Greek history. His works included books on genealogy, mythology and the history of Attica.

Hellenistic General term used to describe the Greek world following the death of Alexander the Great in 323 BC, often applied more specifically to the art of the period between then and the end of the Roman Republic in 31 BC.

Herodotus (c. 484–420 BC) Greek historian, whose account of the Persian Wars is enriched by innumerable digressions and anecdotes, which serve to make him one of the most readable of all ancient authors. His extensive travels and acute powers of observation produced a series of impressions of other peoples and cultures, the accuracy of which modern research has in general largely confirmed.

Hieron I Ruler of Syracuse 478–466 BC and leader of the Greek fleet which defeated the Etruscans at the Battle of Cumae in 474 BC. His court was a center of culture, attracting figures of the eminence of **Aeschylus** and **Pindar**, although he himself, according to **Diodorus Siculus**, was "grasping and violen[t] . . . a man to whom honesty and nobility of character were utterly foreign."

Hittites People who dominated most of **Anatolia** throughout the second millennium BC. After the fall of their empire around 1200 BC the technique of iron smelting, which they had invented and kept secret, spread westwards throughout the Mediterranean world.

Homo erectus (sometimes known as Pithecanthropus) Extinct form of man, living about half a million years ago.

Homo neanderthalensis Later developmen[t] of man, who first appeared around 150,000 B[C]. Neanderthal man had a brain of the same size as modern man, and was the first form of the human race to bury his dead with funerary offerings. As a type he seems to have continued to exist until about 35,000 BC, whe[n] he was replaced by modern man.

Hoplite Greek foot soldier, heavily armed, who fought in tightly packed formations known as phalanxes. It has been estimated tha[t] the armor of a hoplite fully equipped for batt[le] would have weighed around 77 lbs.

Hut-urn Variety of **ash urn** which takes th[e] form of a small round or oval house, generall[y] made of clay but sometimes of bronze, in which the bones and ashes of the dead were placed. It is particularly common in the area around Rome, although examples have been found elsewhere in Early **Iron Age** Italy.

Iliad Epic poem probably composed in its final form in the 8th century BC by the poet traditionally called Homer. It deals with the events preceding the fall of Troy in the late **Bronze Age**, and in particular with the feu[d] between Achilles and Agamemnon, but ther[e] are frequent, if often unconscious, references to the **Iron Age** world in which it was composed.

Indo-European Family of languages which originated in the steppes and spread around 2000 BC westwards to Europe and eastwards to India. As a result almost all modern European languages, and **Sanskrit** and other related Indian languages, share a common origin. Since the discovery of this link by Sir William Jones in 1786 attempts have been made to reconstruct the language of the original "Indo-Europeans" and to work out racial and cultural patterns created by its spread, but in general these have been unsuccessful and the term is best reserved for describing languages.

Monument of an Athenian hoplite

Inhumation Burial of the dead as opposed to cremation, either in a grave dug expressly for the purpose or in a tomb: this can be either a natural chamber, such as a cave, or one specially constructed.

Pre-Villanovan hut-urn

Iron Age In Italy the Iron Age begins around 1000 BC with the arrival of the technique developed by the **Hittites** for smelting iron. As a cultural term it is generally used to describe the peoples of Italy in the period before the development of the Romans, but this is somewhat misleading: the use of iron as prime material for implements, weapons etc. in fact continued until the 19th century and the Industrial Revolution.

Ithyphallic Male figure with exaggeratedly long sexual organ. In primitive art it seems to represent fertility.

Juvenal (?60–?130 AD) Roman satirical poet, about whose life little is known. His 16 satires are among the most biting and inventive in the history of the genre, and have exerted a profound influence on more modern satirists (Swift, Johnson and others). His chief target is the degeneracy of Roman society, for which, according to him, the large numbers of foreigners at Rome are chiefly responsible and he attacks Greeks, Jews, Asians with equal venom. Other objects of attack include homosexuals and, in his longest poem, women.

Knossos The largest palace of the **Minoans**, midway along the north coast of Crete, excavated by Sir Arthur Evans from 1899 to 1935, although further excavation has been conducted there more recently. The technological sophistication and artistic inventiveness revealed by discoveries at Knossos and other Minoan sites are far in advance of any other contemporary Mediterranean culture, although they were to be inherited in large part by the **Mycenaeans**. The palace at Knossos was a multistoried construction, elaborately decorated and continually enlarged from the time of its first construction around 2000 BC to its final destruction around 1400 BC, although retaining throughout its basic ground plan. Frescoes, statuettes and other finds from it provide a vivid picture of Minoan court life.

Lake village Settlement built on pile-supported platforms on the edge of a lake and not, as used to be thought, surrounded by water. The examples in Italy date to the **Neolithic** and Early **Bronze Ages**.

Lanzi, Luigi (1732–1812) Italian archaeologist and linguist, one of the first scholars to attempt a serious study of the Etruscan language. Far more scientific in his approach than most of his contemporaries and predecessors, in 1806 he published at Florence *De' vasi antichi dipinti volgarmente chiamati etruschi*, which attempts to distinguish between the Greek and Etruscan pottery found together in Etruscan tombs.

Laocoön Famous late **Hellenistic** statue of the Trojan priest Laocoön and his two sons being strangled by sea serpents: its discovery in 1506 in the ruins of the Golden House of **Nero** made an immense impact on artists of the Renaissance.

Lares Latin name for the spirits of the dead which watch over their descendants. All Roman houses had a shrine, or Lararium, dedicated to them at which offerings were made, and the domestic practice was extended to the entire town or city which had its own guardian spirits. Their influence was always beneficent, in contrast to the Larvae, the malignant spirits of those dead who could find no rest.

Lawrence, David Herbert (1855–1930) English writer whose account of his visits to Etruscan sites and museums, *Etruscan Places* (first published in 1932), is more valuable as a brilliant piece of travel writing than as a reliable guide to his subject.

Liber Linteus Text inscribed on strips of linen which are then bound together: the **Zagreb Mummy Text** is one of the few surviving examples.

Livy (59 BC–17 AD) Eminent Roman historian, of whose *History of Rome* 35 books survive. Books 1 to 10 are especially valuable for the student of early Italy, covering as they do the history of Rome up to the beginning of the 3rd century BC. Although they are far from reliable, and are based to a great extent on traditional legends that frequently serve to glorify Rome at the expense of her contemporaries (and victims), they preserve for us the Romans' own view of their origins; and as a prose stylist Livy is one of the major figures in Latin literature.

Lucan (39–65 AD) Latin epic poet. Born in Spain, he came to Rome as a child, where his brilliance brought him at an early age into **Nero's** court circle, although a subsequent disagreement with the emperor led to his joining a conspiracy against Nero and committing suicide on its failure. His major work is an epic poem on the civil war between Pompey and Caesar.

Lucumone Etruscan word for king or prince.

Lydia Kingdom in central Asia Minor, the chief city of which in Classical times was Sardis. According to **Herodotus** the Etruscans originally migrated from Lydia.

Maecenas (died 8 BC) Literary adviser and personal friend of **Augustus**, the patron of **Virgil**, Horace and others, Maecenas claimed descent from an Etruscan royal family.

Magna Graecia General term for the Greek colonies of southern Italy and Sicily.

Marcus Aurelius (121–180 AD) Roman emperor from 161 AD to his death, and author of the *Meditations*, written in 12 books in Greek. A Stoic from his early twenties, he retained under all circumstances a belief in the power of reason and an absolute trust in providence.

Mater Matuta Ancient Italic goddess of dawn (hence her name) and also of birth. Her temple at Rome was in the **Forum** Boarium where on 11 June the Matralia, or festival of mothers, was celebrated.

Menhir Standing stone slab on which, in the case of statue menhirs, are carved human attributes, arms, legs and sometimes facial features. Clothing and weapons are also sometimes shown. Most of the examples in western Europe date to the **Neolithic** period, but some **Iron Age** statue menhirs have been found in Liguria.

Statue menhirs from the Magra valley

Menrva Etruscan goddess, the equivalent of Roman Minerva and Greek Athene.

Metope Square slab of stone or terracotta which formed part of the frieze of a **Doric** temple. It was frequently decorated either with paint or with relief sculptures, although in Roman times it was generally used as an ornamental detail in itself, with no added elements.

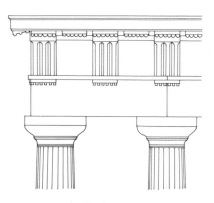

Doric metope

Michelangelo Buonarotti (1475–1564) Most famous of all Renaissance sculptors and painters, whose work was notably influenced by the ancient statues discovered in Rome and elsewhere during his lifetime. He was involved in the restoration of the **Laocoön**.

Minoans and Mycenaeans Cultures of **Bronze Age** Crete and Greece. The Minoans, named by Sir Arthur Evans for Minos, the legendary king of **Knossos**, first appeared in Crete around 2500 BC, and the great period of their culture began around 2000 BC with the construction of the great urban centers dominated by palaces at Knossos, Mallia, Phaistos and Zakro. Their religion was characterized by worship of a mother goddess and their art shows an imagination, variety and love of beauty unique for its period and outstanding in any context. The Mycenaeans, who appeared in southern Greece around 1600 BC and inherited Minoan control of the Aegean on the collapse of Minoan civilization around 1400 BC, show in contrast a greater concern with self-defense: their major centers were fortified citadels, including Mycenae itself, Tiryns and Argos. During the height of their culture, from 1400 BC to the sack of Troy around 1250 BC, the Mycenaeans traded widely throughout the Mediterranean, and established a trading colony in Italy at Taranto. The end of Mycenaean power coincides with the wave of migrations that brought to an end the **Bronze Age** in the Mediterranean around 1100 BC, although memory of them lived on in the **Iliad** and a wide range of Greek myths.

Mother goddess on a Minoan engraved gem

Necropolis Literally city of the dead. An area, generally just outside a town, reserved for burials. The location of such areas outside the walls of the town is typical of most ancient peoples, and particularly striking in the case of the Etruscans, who seem to have lavished more care on the construction of the cities of the dead than on those of the living. Notable examples can be found at Tarquinia and Cerveteri.

Neolithic Last part of the Stone Age, when man had succeeded in domesticating animals and cultivating crops but was still dependent on stone as the material from which tools and weapons were manufactured. In Italy the Neolithic period begins around 5000 BC.

Nero (37–68 AD) Roman emperor from 54 AD to his murder in 68 AD.

Nuraghi Towers, constructed of massive stones, found in Sardinia from the mid-second to the mid-first millennium BC, and giving their name to the so-called Nuraghic culture. The latest examples consist of fortress-like complexes, often surrounded by houses.

Odyssey Epic poem attributed, like the **Iliad**, to Homer, which describes the wanderings of Odysseus on his return journey from the sack of Troy to his native island of Ithaca. Although many of the episodes are clearly imaginary, scholars through the ages have tried to trace Odysseus' journey and identify the lands and peoples he visited.

Orientalizing General term used to describe a stage in the development of Greek art which lasted approximately from 725 to 600 BC, during which Greek painting and sculpture were strongly dominated by styles and motifs (for example the sphinx) of eastern origin. The term is often extended to describe similar stylistic developments in the art of Early **Iron Age** Italy, as for example in the art of the Este people.

Paleolithic Old Stone Age, in which man first appears and manufactures tools for the first time; it began around 2½ million years ago. The first appearance of man in Italy is towards the end of the Mesolithic or Middle Stone Age which acts as transition to the **Neolithic**.

Palilia Festival celebrated annually on 21 April by the Romans to commemorate the founding of their city: it is named for Pales, the Italic goddess of shepherds and flocks.

Pallottino, Massimo (1909–) Eminent contemporary Italian archaeologist, especially known for his work on the Etruscans and other peoples of early Italy.

Pelasgians Term used by Classical writers to refer both to the pre-Indo-European inhabitants of the Mediterranean, and also to specific peoples living in Asia Minor in the Classical period, including the inhabitants of Lemnos. Both **Herodotus** and **Thuycydides** connect the Pelasgians with the Etruscans, but in view of the confusion which seems to have surrounded the term even in ancient times, the information is not very helpful.

Peloponnesian war Long and bitter struggle (431–404 BC) between Athens and her allies on the one hand and the rest of Greece on the other which resulted in the defeat of Athens and the temporary supremacy of Sparta. It forms the subject of the *History* of **Thucydides**.

Phlyax Name given to a type of comic play,

scenes from which appear on Greek vases painted in south Italy during the 4th century BC. The scenes depicted on the vases often show comic versions of heroic themes, and include details which some scholars have used as evidence for contemporary theatrical practices: others, however, are less willing to accept them as depictions of actual stage performances.

Phocea Greek city on the coast of Asia Minor, to the north of Smyrna (modern Izmir). It does not seem to have been settled before the 8th century BC.

Phoenicians Important trading people of the early first millennium BC who occupied the coastal plain of modern Lebanon and Syria: their chief cities were Tyre and Sidon. Their trading contacts extended throughout Asia and westwards as far as Africa, where they founded the colony of **Carthage**. They may even have reached as far north as Britain. The Phoenician alphabet was borrowed by the Greeks, and thereby passed down into the western cultural tradition. In the absence of any Phoenician literature they have survived most vividly in the accounts of their bitter enemies, the Greeks and Romans, and recent discoveries at **Pyrgi** have thrown light on their dealings with the Etruscans.

Phoenician stele from Carthage

Pigorini, Luigi 19th-century Italian anthropologist and prehistorian whose ideas influenced much of early 20th-century work on Italian prehistory, although many of them are now discounted. Rome's prehistoric and ethnological museum is named for him.

Pindar (518–438 BC) Greek lyric poet. Although born near Thebes, he was educated in Athens and his ideas reflect the aristocratic Athenian society of his day. In 476–474 he visited Sicily, where he spent some time at the court of **Hieron** of Syracuse, and composed poems commemorating his victories, including that of the Battle of Cumae.

Piranesi, Giovanni Battista (1720–78) Venetian architect and engraver best known for his etchings of Roman antiquities.

Plato (c. 429–347 BC) One of the greatest of all philosophers, ancient or modern. After the trial and execution of his master Socrates in 399 BC he left Athens, and in the course of his travels spent time in Italy and Sicily, where he established a friendship with Dion, the brother of **Dionysius I** of Syracuse. He returned again in 367 BC to act as tutor to **Dionysius II**, but the attempt to turn the Syracusan ruler into a philosopher-king on the model described in the *Republic* failed, and he returned to Athens in 360 BC.

Polybius (c. 203–c. 120 BC) Greek historian. His account of Rome's rise to power, including the events of the **Punic wars**, was used by **Livy** as a source: what it lacks in elegance of style is compensated for by its impartiality and general accuracy.

Pozzo Burial, often of an urn containing the ashes of the dead, at the foot of a vertical shaft or *pozzo* (the Italian word for well). It was a method frequently used by the Villanovans.

Punic wars Wars between Rome and the **Phoenician** (or Punic) colony of **Carthage**. In the course of the First Punic War (264–241 BC) Carthage lost both Sicily and Sardinia to the Romans, and in the Second (218–201 BC), in spite of Hannibal's successful crossing of the Alps and subsequent victories, the Carthaginians were finally defeated in 202 BC at the Battle of Zama. The so-called Third Punic War of 146 BC was merely a Roman expedition which successfully accomplished its mission of completely destroying the city of Carthage. The Punic Wars represent a decisive turning point in Rome's conquest and control of the Mediterranean.

Pyrgi tablets Three sheets of gold leaf found in 1964 at Pyrgi, one of the ports of ancient Cerveteri, two inscribed in Etruscan and one in **Phoenician**: they have proved immensely valuable both for the study of the Etruscan language and for the history of relations between the Etruscans and the **Carthaginians**.

Quaestor Roman magistrate whose duties were primarily financial: the collection of state revenues, the control of accounts, and the spending of public funds on monuments, public ceremonies and military campaigns. The Samnite equivalent was the *kvaisstor*.

Reithia Goddess of healing who was worshiped by the Este people. A temple dedicated to her has been found just outside Este at Fondo Boratela, together with a number of votive figurines.

Romulus Traditional founder of the city of

Rome, who together with his brother Remus was abandoned on the Palatine hill as a baby and there suckled by a she-wolf.

Sanskrit Language introduced into India by the Aryans, a people who migrated there in the second millennium BC. Sanskrit, which is an **Indo-European** language, was used for sacred literature and ceremonies when it was replaced as the spoken tongue of India.

Scarab seals Sealstones in the shape of the scarab or dung beetle, commonly found in Egypt from the time of the Middle Kingdom (c. 2050 BC). The Egyptians regarded the ball of dung produced by the scarab beetle as a symbol of the sun, and the beetle therefore figures prominently as a religious symbol in Egyptian art. Since the scarab seals are generally inscribed on the underside with a hieroglyphic inscription which often identifies the period to which they belong, they are extremely valuable for dating purposes.

Faience scarab seal from Carthage

Servius (late 4th century AD) Roman grammarian. A teacher of grammar and rhetoric at Rome, he composed a commentary on **Virgil** which included copious notes on historical, mythological and antiquarian references. Although this has not survived in its original form, two versions of it exist which preserve much valuable information, if at times they cast a rather dubious light on the scholarly methods of the late Empire.

Servius Tullius Traditionally the second of the three Etruscan kings of Rome, following **Tarquinius Priscus**: according to most Roman accounts, he was a Latin by birth who had been adopted by Tarquinius Priscus, whose daughter, Tanaquil, he married. The traditional dates of his reign are 578–535 BC, although these have been much disputed, along with most other dates for the early Roman period. According to another version, accepted in his *History of the Etruscans* by the Emperor **Claudius**, Servius Tullius was of Etruscan origin and originally called Mastarna, and became king after a series of events in which Tarquinius was killed, but this alternative account is rejected by most modern scholars.

Silenus Primitive woodland deity whose origins seem to be in Asia Minor. He frequently accompanies **Dionysus** as teacher and companion, and is generally portrayed as a little old man, bald and pot-bellied and generally drunk.

Situla Vessel in the shape of a bucket made of either pottery or bronze. The term has been used to describe an Early **Iron Age** culture whose people produced elaborately decorated bronze situlae. The culture is found in northern Italy, where its chief center was at the modern town of Este in the Veneto, and also to the north in Austria and the east in Yugoslavia. In recent years scholars have begun to explore links between the Situla people and the Etruscans.

Social war (91–88 BC) Revolt on the part of Rome's Italian allies (or *socii*) against Roman authority. It was crushed by prompt military action and by the offer, under the Lex Julia, of Roman citizenship to all Italians, which thereby united the whole of Italy for the first time into a single state. The same offer was made to, and accepted by, the Etruscans, and the end of the Social War therefore marks the formal end of the existence of the Etruscans as a separate people.

Square-mouthed pottery Vessels whose body is circular but whose mouth has been extended and shaped into a square while the clay was still soft. It has given its name to a culture of northern Italy which first appeared there around 4000 BC and lasted about 1,000 years, passing through a number of phases.

Square-mouthed pottery forms

Stele Stone slab or column placed upright and often inscribed or decorated with relief carvings. Stelae were frequently used as grave markers.

Stentinello Neolithic village near Syracuse which produced a type of pottery named for the site. Stentinello ware is found at a number of places in eastern Sicily from 4000 to 3500 BC: it is decorated with elaborate impressed and stamped designs, and with complex hatchings.

Sulla (138–78 BC) Roman politician, who together with his bitter enemy Marius, dominated the political life of Rome in the early 1st century BC. Following the **Social war**, a civil war developed between the two, which continued after Marius' death in 86 BC and was only brought to an end by Sulla's complete victory and massacre of his opponents. The cities of northern Etruria, in particular Chiusi, Volterra and Arezzo, had provided help to Marius' followers and consequently suffered especially ferocious

reprisals at the hands of Sulla's troops. Sulla himself became dictator and introduced a new ultraconservative constitution which did not, however, survive his retirement in 79 BC, the year before his death.

Tarquinius Priscus, Tarquinius Superbus First and third of the three Etruscan kings of Rome. The traditional dates of the reign of Tarquinius Priscus are 616–579 BC, corresponding with the beginning of Etruscan influence at Rome. His name supports the tradition that he came to Rome from Tarquinia, although the family tomb of a family called Tarcna has been found at Cerveteri. Among the innovations with which he was credited was the establishment of games at Rome and the construction of a system of drainage. His successor, **Servius Tullius**, was murdered by Tarquinius Superbus, the son or perhaps grandson of Tarquinius Priscus, who reigned from 534 to 510 BC, the date of the expulsion of the Etruscans from Rome. His achievements included the building of the Capitoline Temple and the draining of the **Forum Romanum** by the construction of the Cloaca Maxima. Etruscan rule at Rome was ended by an uprising provoked by the rape of Lucretia by Tarquinius Superbus' son, Sextus. It must be added that much of the traditional account is clearly based on stories which may well have little or no factual basis, and although the general outline is probably accurate enough, the details are sometimes highly questionable.

Tavoliere Plain in northern Apulia around the modern city of Foggia, where large numbers of **Neolithic** villages have been discovered, dating to around 4000 BC.

Telamon Male figure used in place of a column to support the entablature, or upper level, of a building.

Temple of Zeus at Agrigento with telamones *reconstructed*

Terramara Earth mound of a type found in the Po valley, marking the site of a Middle **Bronze Age** settlement. The Terramare have given their name to the culture represented by

these villages which seems to have arrived in northern Italy from north of the Alps around 1500 BC and is characterized by the use of cremation and a high quality of workmanship in bronze.

Thapsos Late **Bronze Age** trading settlement and cemetery near Syracuse which flourished from 1400 to 1200 BC. Finds indicate connections, probably through trade, with the **Mycenaeans**.

Native (left) and Mycenaean pots from Thapsos

Thucydides (c. 460–399 BC) Greek historian. His *History of the Peloponnesian War* combines a considerable degree of accuracy with a profound grasp of the broader issues involved in the clash between Athens and her enemies, and for most of the time he manages to retain an admirable impartiality. His intellectual, analytical approach is in strong (and deliberate) contrast to the much more discursive style of **Herodotus**.

Tinia Etruscan god, the equivalent of Greek Zeus and Roman Jupiter, and, together with **Uni** and **Menrva**, apparently one of the three chief deities of the Etruscan religion.

Tintinnabulum Small bell, generally of metal.

Trozzella Type of vase produced by the indigenous culture of Apulia. It has long vertical handles which are decorated with small applied wheel-like disks: the word *trozza* means wheel in the Apulian dialect. The round body of the vessel is generally decorated with geometric designs.

Umbro-Sabellian (sometimes known as Osco-Umbrian) Name of the group of **Indo-European** languages, all closely related, spoken by a number of the peoples of the Early **Iron Age** in central Italy. The most northern of these is Umbrian, Sabellic dialects are found in the central region, and Oscan was spoken to the south. All of them are closely related to Latin.

Uni Etruscan goddess, equivalent of Greek Hera and Roman Juno: see **Tinia**.

Vanth Etruscan goddess, who represents, with **Charun**, death and the inevitability of fate. She is depicted with two great wings and generally with an expression that is calm but implacable, in contrast to the far more violent figure of Charun.

Ver sacrum Sacred spring: an Italic custom whereby children born in certain years were, when they were grown up, sent away from their home town and required to found a new city, thereby diffusing their culture while relieving overpopulation. Although the custom was chiefly practiced by the Italic tribes, it also existed at Rome: the last occasion was during the Second **Punic war** when children born in 217 BC left Rome in 195–194 BC.

Vesta Latin goddess of the hearth and its fire. Although she corresponds to the Greek goddess Hestia, Vesta plays a more important role than her Greek equivalent. Besides the celebration of her cult at the hearth of every home, she was also worshiped by the state, and the round temple dedicated to her stood in the center of the **Forum Romanum**. Her six priestesses were known as the Vestal Virgins.

Villa Giulia Country villa of Pope Julius III, built from 1551 to 1553 to a design by Vignola. The villa now houses the Museo Nazionale di Villa Giulia, containing pre-Roman antiquities from southern Etruria, Umbria and Latium: among the most important of its contents are the finds from the Praeneste tombs and the terracotta temple sculptures from Veii.

Virgil (70–19 BC) Perhaps the greatest of all Roman poets, and a major influence in the development of western literature. His first two works, the ten *Eclogues* (or *Bucolics*) and the four books of the *Georgics*, reflect his interest in the natural world and his belief that the best life is that of the countryman. In his last and most complex work, the **Aeneid**, Virgil was faced with the task of providing Rome with an epic poem worthy to stand beside the **Iliad** and the **Odyssey** while at the same time responding to the patriotic spirit of the new Rome of **Augustus**. Although he did not live to finish it, and in fact left instructions in his will that it should be destroyed, the *Aeneid* remains a profoundly moving study of the nature of human destiny and personal responsibility.

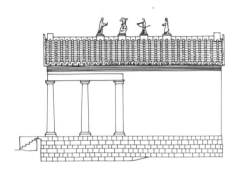

Temple of Apollo at Veii reconstructed with Vulca's statues

Vulca Etruscan sculptor, the only one whose name is mentioned by Roman writers, according to whom he was summoned from his home city of Veii to provide the statues and terracotta decorations for the Temple of Jupiter on the Capitoline at Rome. He is generally credited with the terracotta statues found at Veii, dating to the late 6th century, which are now in the **Villa Giulia**.

Vulcan Roman and Italic god of fire and the forge, corresponding to the Greek Hephaestus.

Winckelmann, Johannes (1717–68) Sometimes called the Father of Archaeology, he was one of the first scholars to base his study of ancient art on the objects themselves rather than on ancient authors. His major work, the *History of Ancient Art*, first appeared in 1763 and consists of an investigation into the nature of the art of the Egyptians, Greeks, Etruscans, Romans and other ancient peoples, and a detailed chronological study of Greek art. In spite of the large numbers of new discoveries being made almost daily at Herculaneum and Pompeii, which Winckelmann incorporated in his work, his conclusions have inevitably been outdated by the finds of the last two centuries. Nonetheless his work was immensely valuable in demonstrating the importance of detailed analysis of the works of art themselves.

Xenophon (c. 430–c. 354 BC) Greek historian. A number of his works have survived, including the *Hellenica*, a history of Greece which begins at the point where **Thucydides** ends, in 411 BC, the *Anabasis*, an account of his adventures in Persia, and works on horsemanship, hunting and the running of an estate. He is one of the writers cited by **Annio of Viterbo**, who forged appropriate "extracts."

Zagreb Mummy Text Longest surviving Etruscan inscription, originally written on a **Liber Linteus** which was subsequently used as the winding cloth of a mummy. It seems to be a kind of liturgical calendar.

INDEX